PARADOX
AND
COUNTERPARADOX

PARADOX
AND
COUNTERPARADOX

*A New Model in the Therapy of the
Family in Schizophrenic Transaction*

MARA SELVINI PALAZZOLI, M.D.
LUIGI BOSCOLO, M.D.
GIANFRANCO CECCHIN, M.D.
GIULIANA PRATA, M.D.

translated by Elisabeth V. Burt

NEW YORK • JASON ARONSON • LONDON

ISBN 0-87668-337-5

L.C. No: 78-60662

Originally published in Italy by Feltrinelli Editore, Milan, 1975.

CONTENTS

FOREWORD

Paradox and Counterparadox demonstrates the revolutionary thrust of the new paradigm of family therapy. Its authors have been working as a team for approximately eight years, and have rightly been hailed as pioneers in the treatment of severe psychiatric conditions which have until now defied most therapeutic endeavors.

We read at one point in the book that its senior author, the Milanese psychoanalyst Mara Selvini Palazzoli, is seen as a wizard in certain circles of patients and colleagues, i.e. as someone who can cure a patient and his family in one mere hour. Understandably, the author rejects such an imputation. And yet—someone like myself, who has followed Doctor Selvini's career and writings over the years, has a hard time not believing in at least a little wizardry.

Approximately ten years ago she published in Italian a book on her psychoanalytic experiences with patients suffering from anorexia nervosa. In that book she showed an unusual insight into the intrapsychic dynamics and object relations of her anorectic girls and, in spite of her investment, in many cases, of more than one hundred individual sessions, reported honestly on her modest therapeutic successes. That book is now available in English (*Self-Starvation*, Jason Aronson, 1978) with several additional chapters covering subsequent family therapy with these patients. And here, all of a sudden, wizardry seemed to operate: in the approximately one dozen families seen in conjoint sessions, the anorexia of the presenting patient disappeared for good after no more (and often far fewer) than fifteen sessions, while the whole family changed deeply and lastingly.

Paradox and Counterparadox, a natural successor to her book on anorexia, increases rather than decreases this impression of wizardry. We learn that she and her team, having become a little bored with anorectic families (who always present the same dynamics), have now turned to families with schizo-phrenic members. So far their successes with "schizo-present" families have been just as striking as with families of anorectics. The authors limit these psychotic families to a total of twenty sessions spaced approximately a month apart. However, families with seriously chronic patients, damaged by long hospitalizations, have so far been excluded.

A thorough reading of this book reveals the "wizardry" to have a solid theoretical base. This base was laid by Gregory Bateson, Jay Haley, Paul Watzlawick, Harley Shands, and others who took seriously the cybernetic revolution of our century and who developed a "transactional epistemology" that replaces a monocausal, linear model with a circular model. This circular model has sensitized us to those paradoxes which inhere in healthy as well as pathological relationships, paradoxes which normally elude us because we lack the linguistic tools to grasp them.

For we all remain, willy-nilly, bound up with a language which programs us more or less for a monocausal, linear way of thinking. Even so, most of us can somehow cope with our transactional world, while many—perhaps all—families with schizophrenic members seem unable to do so. For they get caught up in formidable "relationship traps" and hence get lost in a relational and communicational labyrinth sans exit. The consequences are deepest mutual alienation, exploitation and counterexploitation, and relational and developmental stagnation.

Paradoxical injunctions, as introduced into family therapy by Haley, Watzlawick, and others, offer a therapeutic strategy for entering such labyrinths. This strategy is at the heart of Doctor Selvini's and her team's therapeutic endeavors. They acquaint us here with a potent therapeutic instrument that utilizes two main elements:

1. The therapists establish a positive relationship with all family members. To do so, they accept and "connote positively" anything the family offers, avoiding even the faintest hint which might be construed as a moralizing stance or accusation, or which might otherwise induce anxiety, shame, or guilt.
2. The therapists aim at a radical reshuffling of the relational forces operating in these families: they shake the family out of its destructive clinch, as it were, and try to give all members a new chance to pursue their own individuation and separation.

Like any other potent instrument, such injunctions can harm as well as help. To be therapeutic, careful preparation, extensive experience in family therapy, and empathy toward all family members are needed. In addition, Dr. Selvini and her team demonstrate one more quality that seems indispensable: the courage to develop and adopt new models and concepts when those one has learned no longer suffice.

Helm Stierlin, M.D.

PREFACE

This book is the report of a research program devised by the group of coauthors at the end of 1971 and initiated in early January 1972. It concerns therapeutic work conducted with fifteen families, five of which presented children age five to seven with serious psychotic behavior, and ten of which presented subjects between ten and twenty-two who had been diagnosed as acute schizophrenics of relatively recent onset and had received no institutional treatment.

In order to proceed gradually we have for the present excluded families with chronic patients who already have a history of institutional treatment. To this end we have relied upon the cooperation of colleagues whose generous assistance has enabled us to put our research into effect.

The publication of this preliminary report is in response to the pressing requests we have received from numerous quarters to publicize the method and effects of our type of work. We are acceding to these requests despite the fact that publication is undoubtedly premature, in that for a number of families which have displayed rapid and dramatic changes there has not been sufficient time for an adequately prolonged follow-up control.

We continue to use, in the interests of common understanding, the Bleulerian term *schizophrenia*, by now universally employed, signifying with this, however, not the illness of an individual, but a particular communication pattern inseparable from the communication patterns observable in the natural group in which it occurs: in our case the family in schizophrenic transaction.

Our work has been characterized by the attempt to be methodologically consistent, deriving therapeutic applications strictly in accordance with the chosen conceptual model.

We are of the opinion that the most important aspect of this first report is the exposition of the therapeutic interventions we have devised. In other words, we believe it more interesting for the reader to see what we *do* rather than what we *think* when confronted with schizophrenic interaction. Notwithstanding, however, we have in the second part of the volume deemed it necessary to present our ideas in order to render our actions comprehensible.

We thank all our friends who have encouraged and helped us: psychologists, psychiatrists, and social workers who by encouraging families to seek family treatment have allowed us to put our research plans into practice. We wish to express our gratitude to Dr. Paul Watzlawick, whose friendly interest in our work has been a constant encouragement and stimulus to us, and, finally, to Mrs. Enrica Dal Pont Solbiati for her generous assistance in putting the manuscript in order.

Milan, 31 October 1974.

Part I

chapter 1

INTRODUCTION

This book deals with experimental research conducted by our team in an attempt to establish the validity of a working hypothesis derived from the models offered by cybernetics and communication theory. This hypothesis is, that the family is a self-regulating system which controls itself according to rules formed over a period of time through a process of trial and error.

The central idea of this hypothesis is that every natural-group-with-history, of which the family is a fundamental example (work teams, spontaneous communities, and managerial groups are others), comes to exist through a period of time through a series of transactions and corrective feedbacks. These assay what is permitted and what is not permitted in the relationship, until the natural group becomes a systemic unit held together by rules peculiar to it alone. These rules are related to the transactions which occur in the natural group, transactions which have the quality of communication, whether on the verbal or nonverbal level. In fact, according to the axioms of *Pragmatics of Human Communication* (Watzlawick, Beavin, and Jackson 1967) every behavior is a communication which, in its turn, automatically provokes a feedback consisting of another behavior-communication. Following this hypothesis, one arrives at still another hypothesis: families in which one or more members present behaviors traditionally diagnosed as "pathological," are held together by transactions and, therefore, by rules peculiar to the pathology. Hence the behavior-communications and the behavior-responses will have such characteristics which maintain the rules and, thereby, the pathological transaction. Since the symptomatic behavior is part of the transactional pattern peculiar to the system in which it occurs, the way to eliminate the symptoms is to change the rules. The methods invented with this goal in mind are described in Part Three of this book.

Our results have indicated that when we are able to discover and change one fundamental rule, pathological behavior quickly disappears. This has led us to accept the idea proposed by Rabkin: "In nature, happenings of radical importance sometimes take place suddenly when a fundamental rule of a system is changed" (1972, p. 97). Rabkin proposes the term *saltology* (from the Latin *saltus*, meaning "leap") for the scientific study of these phenomena.

Saltology finds its correspondence in General Systems Theory, whose proponents speak of p_s as being the point of a system at which the maximum number of functions essential to its existence converge, and which, if modified, effects the maximum change with a minimal expense of energy. On the other hand, experience has shown us the power of systems, much greater when pathological, to maintain and sustain the rules they have created over a period of time through the process of trial and error and through the stochastic process (a sort of memorization of proven solutions).

From General Systems Theory, we know that every living system is characterized by two apparently contradictory functions: the homeostatic tendency on one hand, and the capacity for transformation on the other. The interplay of these seemingly antithetical functions maintains the system in a provisional equilibrium whose instability guarantees evolution and creativity.

In pathological systems, however, one observes the increasingly rigid tendency to compulsively repeat proven solutions in order to maintain the homeostasis. After having obtained a number of rapid changes in the treatment of families with anorectic patients, we chose as our subject of study the family characterized by schizophrenic transaction. The family of the anorectic, with its behavior redundancies and rigid rules, could be compared to an extremely mechanistic and rigidly planned cybernetic circuit. The family of the psychotic, however, displayed not only even greater rigidities, but transactional patterns of enormous complexity and an impressive variety and inventiveness in maintaining the schzophrenic game.

The acceptance of these hypotheses requires an epistemological change, in the original sense of the Greek verb *epistamai*, which means to put oneself "over" or "higher" in order to better observe something. To do this, we must abandon the causal-mechanistic view of phenomena, which has dominated the sciences until recent times, and adopt a systemic orientation. With this new orientation, the therapist should be able to see the members of the family as elements in a circuit of interaction. None of the members of the circuit have unidirectional power over the whole, although the behavior of any one of the members of the family inevitably influences the behavior of the others. At the same time, it is epistemologically incorrect to consider the behavior of one individual the *cause* of the behavior of the others. This is because every member influences the others, but is in turn influenced by them. The individual acts upon the system, but is at the same time influenced by the communications he receives from it.

One particularly clear example of this phenomenon can be found in the neurohormonal field. In the system of the human body, the *hypophisis,* for instance, certainly acts upon the system, but it is in turn influenced by all information from the system, and therefore does not have any unidirectional power. Thus, every family transaction is a series of behavior-responses which, in their turn, influence other behavior-responses, and so on.

Therefore, saying that the behavior of one individual is the *cause* of the behavior of other individuals is an epistemological error. This error derives from the arbitrary punctuation which isolates such behavior from the pragmatic context of preceding behaviors which can be traced back to infinity. Even a behavior which, in various ways, reduces its apparent victim to impotence is not a "behavior-power," but rather a "behavior-response." And yet, whoever thinks of himself as being in the "superior" position believes himself the one with power, just as the one in the "inferior" position thinks of himself as the one without it.

We, however, know these convictions to be wrong: the power belongs to neither the one nor the other. *The power is only in the rules of the game* which cannot be changed by the people involved in it. Our experience has led us to the conviction that to continue looking at phenomena according to the causal model is a serious impediment to the understanding of the family game, and therefore renders impotent whoever attempts to change it.

In other fields of science, the acceptance of this new epistemological model, based mainly on the concept of feedback, has permitted enormous progress to the point of sending man to the moon. In the behavioral sciences, however, this new epistemology was not introduced until the 1950s, mainly by the studies of Gregory Bateson and his team at Palo Alto, California. Their major interest was the study of communication, which was conducted using data and observations derived from various sources: hypnosis, animal training, communication in schizophrenic and neurotic subjects, studies of popular movies, the nature of games, fantasy, play, paradox, etc. The most striking and innovating element of this research project, which took place in the decade 1952-1962, was the introduction of certain concepts from Whitehead and Russell's *Principia Mathematica*, a work which led to a new logic, one distinguished from Aristotelian logic by centrality of the concept of "function."

Here the traditional logic failed completely: it believed that there was only one form of single proposition, namely, the form which ascribes a predicate to a subject; this is the appropriate form in assigning the qualities of a given thing—we may say "this is round, and red, and so on." Grammar favours this form, but philosophically it is so far from universal that it is not even very common. If we say "this thing is bigger than that," we are not assigning a mere quality of "this," but a relation of "this" on "that." We might express the same fact by saying "that thing is smaller than this," where grammatically the subject is changed. Thus propositions stating that two things have a certain relation have a different form from subject-predicate proposition, and the failure to perceive this difference or to allow for it has been the source of many errors in traditional metaphysics. The belief or unconscious conviction that all propositions are of the subject-predicate form—in other words, that every fact consists in something having some quality—has rendered most philosophers incapable of giving any account of the world of science and daily life. [Russell 1960, p. 42]

In 1956 the Palo Alto group published "Toward a Theory of Schizophrenia," based on Russell's Theory of Logical Types. The central thesis of this theory is that there is a discontinuity between a class and its members. The class cannot be a member of itself, nor can one of the members represent the class, because the term used for the class is of a different level of abstraction than the terms used for its members. According to the hypothesis of Bateson and his team, when this discontinuity is not respected in human relations, paradoxes of the Russellian type appear with pathological consequences This led to the forumulation of the theory of the double bind as a paradoxical communication mostly present in the families of schizophrenic patients.

The Palo Alto group came to consider schizophrenia a "conflict of logical types," the result of characteristic repetitive patterns of communication. In 1967, Watzlawick, Beavin, and Jackson published *Pragmatics of Human Communication*, which traced out the dimensions of a new science of communication: the ways in which each person influences others through the message character of his behavior (and therefore of the ways in which each person confirms, refuses, or disconfirms others who may have a relationship with him).

This work offered us the proper instruments for the analysis of communication: the concept of context as matrix of meanings; the notion of the coexistence of two languages, the analogic and the digital; the concept of punctuation in interaction; the concept of the necessity to define the relationship and the various verbal and nonverbal levels which can be used to define it; the notion of symmetrical and complementary positions in relationships; and the fundamental notion of symptomatic and therapeutic paradox. As far as paradoxes are concerned, we can say that our research has shown how the family in schizophrenic transaction sustains its game through an intricacy of paradoxes which can only be undone by counterparadoxes in the context of therapy.

This new epistemology opens new horizons, both theoretical and practical. In particular, it permits us to look at the symptom as a phenomenon consistent with the transactional patterns specific to the group. Finally, this new epistemology transcends those Cartesian dualisms whose persistence is by now a hindrance rather than a help to scientific progress. Since in a systemic circuit each element interacts with its totality, any dichotomies, such as body-mind or conscious-unconscious, lose their meaning.

chapter 2

WORKING METHOD

The Institute for Family Study, organized by Mara Selvini Palazzoli, began its activity in Milan, Italy, May 1967.

The work began in the face of many obstacles, such as the difficulty of finding and motivating families to treatment in a culturally unprepared and often hostile milieu. The team itself was made up of only two cotherapists, who, although expert in individual and group psychotherapy, were totally inexperienced in family work.

For various reasons related to the situation of institutional psychiatry in Italy, it was decided to create a center completely independent of public institutions. Several pressures can disturb a team: the timetable for the publication of data, the imposition of new members on a team, the instrumentalization of the research for political and propaganda purposes.

This decision of autonomy, although it presents fundamental advantages, also implies certain disadvantages not to be ignored: the difficulty in finding specific cases, the lack of funds to meet expenses. This second disadvantage has been resolved by working only part-time with a reduced number of families who pay a fee according to their means. The Institute was legally founded as a nonprofit organization, and the fees coming from the families are used to pay the expenses of running the Institute. The members of the team receive no compensation for their work with the families.

Beginning in 1972, the number of families applying to the Institute continually increased, until more applied than the Institute could accept for treatment. This made it possible to select cases and focus research on particular types of illnesses. Among these last was a study concerning families of patients with anorexia nervosa, which was reported in the fourth part of the English edition of *Self-Starvation: From the Intrapsychic to the Transpersonal Approach to Anorexia Nervosa* (1974).

Since families receiving psychotherapy must pay a fee according to their means,[1] one can deduce that their motivation is comparable to that of patients who request individual therapy. The paying of a fee, in fact, presupposes a certain motivation in the client and protects his independence in the therapeutic situation. The fee constitutes an important element which differentiates our work from that carried out in the institutional setting.

The team, which during 1970 and 1971 had grown progressively until it for a short time included eight members, underwent various vicissitudes, which ended in a division and reorganization. The present research team was formed at the end of 1971. It is made up of four members, the authors of this book, two men and two women, all psychiatrists. This combination permits the use in therapeutic work of a heterosexual couple, always backed up by the other pair of colleagues in the observation room.

The use of the therapeutic heterosexual couple is another important aspect of the Institute's work: a more "physiological" equilibrium is brought about between the two cotherapists, and between them and the family. Moreover, certain redundancies in the initial interaction of the family with one or the other of the therapists can help the team understand certain rules of the family game.

Thus in the case of the family traditionally dominated by women, the members, or certain members, of the family will immediately show a tendency to direct themselves toward the female therapist, apparently ignoring her partner. The use of the heterosexual couple has also given us the advantage of avoiding falling into certain cultural sexual stereotypes inevitably shared by the therapists. In discussing family sessions, we have often observed the completely contradictory impressions expressed by the two therapists in regard to the couple and the tendency to view moralistically the interaction between the two:

"How could he marry a woman like that!"

"What are you talking about? He's the one who provokes her. Didn't you notice? He was even doing it with me!"

Being aware of this phenomenon helped us accede to the systemic model against the strongly rooted tendency to make arbitrary punctuation and causal interpretations.

The heterosexual therapeutic couples are not fixed, but interchange with every new family in alternating combinations, the only requirement being that each member of the team work equal hours as therapist and as observer. This procedure has permitted us to observe the variables inherent in the personality of each therapist, in the reciprocal relationships between the therapists, and in the work style developed by each couple. This approach allows us to realize that success in therapy is not dependent upon the charismatic personality of one or the other of the therapists, but rather upon the method followed. In truth, *if the method is correct, no charisma whatsoever is needed.*

This is the procedure we have chosen and which has proven the most efficient. Needless to say, we do not consider it the only one possible. Certainly a single therapist, with sufficient experience, can work with the family. But we feel it is indispensable for him to have live supervision.

Since our first contact with the family occurs over the telephone, we have established special hours for these calls so that one of the therapists is always available to talk at length if necessary, thus avoiding errors and misunderstandings due to shortness of time. We can never stress enough the fact that therapy begins with the first telephone call. During the conversation many phenomena can be noted: peculiarities of communication, tone of voice, peremptory demands for all kinds of information, immediate attempts to manipulate by trying to make the appointment for a particular day or hour, attempts to reverse roles so that it appears as if it were the therapist searching for patients and not the family asking for help. This precision and attention to detail is fundamental in the beginning of any therapeutic relationship, but above all with the family in schizophrenic transaction.

As we will see later, giving in to even the simplest and most apparently "reasonable" request of the family can weaken the therapeutic role and change the context of the therapy.

Except for very particular cases, we are even against making "emergency" appointments. We also refuse the attempts of some parents to obtain preliminary appointments without the presence of the child. Here we do make exceptions of parents of children under three years of age, or of older children who have been traumatized by previous negative psychiatric experiences. In such cases we see only the parents in order to decide if we can reasonably expect results for the family through the therapy of the couple alone.

In all other cases, above all with families presenting a patient designated as schizophrenic, the first session includes all the members of the immediate family living together. Later, if the therapy requires it, it is the therapists who decide on an eventual change in the make-up of the family group. However, our latest experiences have taught us to break the family group only in exceptional cases, since such a move is felt by the family as threatening and can lead to interruption of the therapy. The information obtained during the first telephone contact is recorded on the standard chart below:

Name of the referring person _____ *Date of call* _____
Address of family _____
Name, age, education, religion and profession:
of the father _____
of the mother _____
of children in order of birth _____
Date of marriage _____
Other members of the household and their relationship
Problem _____

Who called _____

*Observations*_____

*Information from the referring person*_____

Occasionally, the telephone contact has been preceded by a discussion with the referring doctor, and any pertinent information obtained from this discussion is added to the chart. Since the first session may take place after a long period of time, this registered information is indispensable.

The sessions take place in a room which is especially furnished with several small armchairs, a soundproofed ceiling, and a large one-way mirror. A microphone, which is attached to the recorder located in the adjoining observation room, is placed in the center of a ceiling lamp. The family is told of our team approach. We explain the use of the microphone and of the one-way mirror, behind which, we tell them, are two colleagues who assist us in our work and with whom we discuss the case before the conclusion of each session.

Each session can be divided into five parts:

1. During *the presession,* the therapists meet to read either the family's chart, if this is to be the first meeting, or the report of the previous session.

2. *The session* lasts about an hour, during which time the therapists solicit a certain amount of information from the family; they are interested not only in concrete information but also in the way information is given, which indicates the transactional style of the family. While the families in schizophrenic transaction attempt to give us the lowest possible level of information, they cannot avoid showing us their particular ways of communicating. The behavior of the therapists is designed to provoke interaction between various members of the family, allowing us to observe sequences, verbal and nonverbal messages, and any redundancies indicating the existence of secret rules. The therapists refrain from pointing out these observations to the family, as well as from making comments until the conclusion of the session.

If the observers note that the therapists are becoming

confused or disoriented by some maneuver of the family, they may knock on the door to call one of the therapists into the observation room, where they try to clarify the situation or suggest new methods of approach. It may also happen that one of the therapists comes out of the room spontaneously to seek advice from the observers while the other continues the session.

3. *The discussion of the session* occurs in a room reserved exclusively for this use. The two therapists and the two observers unite to discuss the session and how to conclude it.

4. In *the conclusion of the session*, the two therapists rejoin the family in order to make a brief comment and prescription, which is to be paradoxical, with rare exceptions which will be explained later. If this has been the first meeting, the therapists tell the family whether or not a psychotherapeutic treatment is indicated. If the conclusion is for therapy, and the family accepts, the fee and number of sessions are agreed upon.

Our most recent procedure has been to fix ten sessions at about monthly intervals. Originally we made weekly sessions, which was then the common practice, but to accommodate families who had to travel very long distances (some as far as 300 miles) we began to give appointments at longer intervals and, surprisingly, found this schedule to be more effective. This casual observation led us to extend this practice to all families, having seen that paradoxical prescriptions exercised a greater "impact" on the family system if they were carried out for a longer period of time.

Furthermore, as a result of repeated empirical observation, we were able to form a theoretical hypothesis regarding the t_s or time of the system. Every system, as is well known, is not only characterized by a p_s, or nodal point, which is peculiar to the system, but also by its own "time": By its very nature a system consists of an interaction, and this means that a sequential process of action and reaction has to take place before we are able to describe any state of the system *or any change of state*" (Lennard and Bernstein 1960).

It is understood that in rigid homeostatic systems, the t_s

necessary for change is far greater than in flexible morphogenetic systems. The introduction into a system of an unexpected and unsettling communication, such as a paradoxical intervention, needs a span of time specific to that system so that it can organize, on the basis of the actions and reactions of its individual components, a new way of functioning.

From the therapeutic point of view, we can observe that when the behavior of one member of the family changes as a result of an effective intervention, it takes a certain span of time before a corrective maneuver in another member or members becomes exasperated to the point of being evident (for an example see the case presented in chapter 17).

Case by case, session by session, it is the task of the team to decide upon the length of the interval, which may vary anywhere from two weeks to several months. At times this interval is punctuated by alarming telephone calls from the family, which insists upon an earlier session. Obviously we do not give in to these attempts. This is for us a further demonstration that the shortening of an interval acts in favor of family resistance. To give in to the request condemns the therapists to impotence because the new phenomena have not yet fully revealed themselves.

Our decision to limit the number of sessions to ten was determined by our conviction that with these families we would have to provoke changes rapidly or miss the opportunity for change entirely! In addition, the family is on the one hand made to feel strongly responsible for results because of the brevity of the treatment and on the other hand is reassured as to duration and cost. With two of the families treated to date, at the conclusion of ten sessions, we have agreed to a second cycle of ten sessions. We have never exceeded the total of twenty sessions.

We could, therefore, paradoxically define this method of work as a *long brief therapy*. It is *brief* considering the time dedicated by the therapists to working directly with the family, and *long* in respect to the time needed by the family to organize the transformation.

5. When the family has left, the team unites to discuss the family's reaction to the comment or prescription, to formulate

and to write *the synthesis of the session.* If there have been especially
important transactions, these are written down verbatim. In
case of doubt, the tapes of the session can be played back.

The procedure we have thus described entails, as can easily
be seen, a great deal of time. In especially difficult sessions,
three to four hours have been sometimes necessary. Furthermore, this type of work demands a harmonious group which is
not disturbed by competition or factions, whose members
share a reciprocal respect and willingness to accept observations and suggestions. The number of members of the group is
also important. If the team is too small, it has difficulty in
controlling the power of the schizophrenic play. If it is too
large, important points can get lost in long and rambling
discussions and moreover the danger of competition and of the
forming of cliques is greater. In our experience, four members
seem the best combination. We repeat our conviction that an
extremely difficult therapy, such as that of the family in
schizophrenic transaction, can be confronted only by a team
free from internal strife. The least competitive urge within the
team, in fact, immediately instrumentalizes the problems of
the family as a pretext for argument within the group. Teams
created by the authorities of institutions are especially prone
to this danger.

We also feel that continual supervision by the two colleagues
in the observation room is indispensable. External as they are
to what occurs in the treatment room, they are less easily
drawn into the play and can observe in perspective, in a global
manner as it were, as if they were spectators watching a
football match from the grandstands. The game on the field is
always better grasped by the observers than by the protago-
nists themselves. In conclusion, we can say that a therapeutic
team dedicated to research is a delicate instrument, exposed to
many hazards, internal as well as external. One of the greatest
hazards comes from the families themselves, especially until
the team is sufficiently experienced. At the beginning of our
work with these families, it often happened that we were taken
in by the family's game to the point that our resulting

frustration and anger became transferred to the relationship between ourselves.

We will present in chapters 3 and 4 our conception of the schizophrenic game. In the remainder of the book we will describe our tactics and the many trials and errors through which we have arrived at this conception.

Part II

Part II

chapter 3

THE COUPLE AND THE FAMILY
IN SCHIZOPHRENIC TRANSACTION

Jay Haley, in "The Family with a Schizophrenic Patient: a Model System" (1959), is the first to point out the particular reluctance of each member of such a family to admit either that his behavior is controlled and influenced by the other members of the family, or that he himself regulates their behavior. Characteristically, the members of such a family avoid making any definition of their relationships with one another.

This fundamental observation, which has been confirmed in our experience, has led us to the hypothesis that the family in schizophrenic transaction is a natural group internally regulated by a symmetry which is exasperated to the point that each member perceives its open declaration as extremely dangerous. Therefore, everyone cooperates in keeping it hidden.

As a counterexample, let us observe a relationship which openly shows symmetry. Here each member of the couple, while showing openly his urge to prevail, implicitly accepts the possibility of his own failure. This is a risk the members of the family in schizophrenic transaction cannot afford to take.

In the interaction of a couple in which the symmetry is open, the mode of interaction is rejection. Each of the partners rejects the definition of the relationship made by the other. Certainly, for each of the two, the rejection of the other is a blow, but rather than being unbearable, this rejection is foreseen, and serves as a stimulus for a counterattack. Each of the two boldly exposes himself to the other and firmly proceeds in the escalation of rejection and redefinition. This game can go on forever, but it can also run the risk of schismatic process: abandonment of the field by one of the couple, and thereby the loss of the adversary and, thus, the game; physical violence; and even murder.

Let us go back to the couples we define as being in schizophrenic transaction and try to understand how symmetry remains hidden.

Living together inevitably implies the setting up of a system of learning: how to learn to live together. This "how to" is none other than a series of trials and errors through which the two will *learn to learn*, that is, they will find the solutions to the major problem which concerns them: how to live together. However, each of the two comes from a different learning system regulated by certain solutions which make up part of his or her stochastic storehouse. These solutions will inevitably enter into the play of the building up of the new system, conditioning it in various ways. Thus we can say that the trials and errors which go into the new system of learning do not come from a tabula rasa, but rather from the solutions of previous learning systems.

The observations made by our team, especially in the case of therapy of families with psychotic children, of the families of the paternal and maternal grandparents have fully confirmed the assertion of Bowen that "at least three generations are needed to produce a schizophrenic" (1960, p. 352). In these families of the paternal and maternal grandparents, the solutions found for the problem of how to live together express already a particular rigidity and repetitiveness. In the second generation, that is, in the young couple, in addition to the dysfunctional solutions adopted by the first generation, we observe another dysfunction of fundamental importance: the reluctance to expose oneself to rejection.

Each of the two has started out with an enormous desire to receive confirmation, a desire all the more intense as it is chronically frustrated. In fact, already in the family of the first generation, the battle for the definition of the relationship, characteristic of the human being, has reached the point in which the parents act as if the rendering of approval were a sign of weakness. In other words, if someone does something well, it is clear that he only does so in order to receive praise or approval. In such a case, the rendering of approval or praise would mean giving in to his expectations, putting oneself "down," and sustaining a loss of prestige and authority.

To maintain this position of prestige and authority, it is necessary to withhold approval, to find something to criticize or make fun of: "Yes, but you could have done better"; "Fine, but the next time. . . ."

What happens then to the two partners when, from their original learning contexts, they attempt to build a new one? Both will be driven by the same need and by the same tension. This time each one has to make it, has to finally be able to define the relationship and receive confirmation. But whom has he chosen as a partner in this enterprise? As we have seen, time and time again, a "difficult" partner, one who shares the very same problems.

To explain this phenomenon we refer to Bateson:

> Problems of this general type are frequent in psychiatry, and can perhaps only be resolved by a model in which, under certain circumstances, the organism's discomfort activates a positive feedback loop to *increase* the behavior which preceded the discomfort. Such positive feedback would provide a verification that it was really that particular behavior which brought about the discomfort and might increase the discomfort up to some threshold level at which change becomes possible. It will be noted that the possible existence of such a positive feedback loop, which will cause a runaway in the direction of increasing discomfort up to some threshold (which might be on the other side of death), is not included in conventional theories of learning. *But a tendency to verify the unpleasant by seeking repeated experience of it is a common human*

trait. It is perhaps what Freud called the "death instinct."
[Bateson 1972, pp. 327-328; italics ours]

Our experience has led us to consider the state of
discomfort, here described by Bateson, as the consequence of a
person's finding himself "down" when he has tried to be "up"
in the effort to define the relationship. Let it be clear that we
are not talking about the effort to control other persons, but
rather about the effort to control the relationship.

Man is a being who will not easily accept this kind of defeat;
he will return compulsively to the battlefield to try again and
again. He even carries on the same battle with God, as we are
taught in the first book of Genesis, when Adam and Eve ask
why they should not eat the fruits of the tree. It is man's
hubris[2] which led to his banishment from the paradise of
complementarity with his creator, which he had initially
recognized and gladly accepted.

In this sense, the common human characteristic of which
Bateson speaks could be hubris, "the pretention to succeed"
one day or another, even at the price of death. It is by following
this line of hubris, already exaggerated by their respective
original learning systems, that each member of our couple
chooses a "difficult" partner. And it is exactly because of this
hubris that each wants to repeat the challenge; that each
presumes to succeed.

We can observe that the positions of the two in the
relationship are identical and symmetrical. Each yearns
desperately to gain control of the definition of the relationship,
and repeatedly and compulsively tests his position, thus
constantly running the risk of defeat.

However, hubris, that exasperated pride, has taken up its
abode in each member of the couple, and can admit no defeat.
Failure, or even its possibility, becomes unbearable, and must
be prevented at any cost. Withdrawing from the conflict does
not present itself as a solution, for this would be the same as
admitting defeat. The battle must go on, but with no risk for
the adversaries. Thus, they choose the only solution: the
avoidance of any definition of the relationship. *Each must*

disqualify his own definition of the relationship before the other has the chance to do it.

Thus the great game begins and its secret rules are formed. Communication between the two becomes more and more cryptic in their mutual attempt to avoid exposure. They learn how to skillfully avoid any *patent* contradiction and become expert in the use of the paradox, taking advantage of that possibility, specific to man, to communicate simultaneously on the verbal and the nonverbal level, jumping from one logical class to a member of that class, as if they were the same thing, thus becoming acrobats in the world of the Russellian paradox.

The communicational maneuvers which characterize schizophrenic transaction are well known: partial or total disqualification of the message, sidestepping of the main issue, change of subject, non sequitur, amnesia, and finally, the supreme maneuver of disconfirmation.

When we use the term *disconfirmation,* we are speaking of the type of response made by one of the interlocutors to the definition which the other tries to give of himself in the relationship. This reply is neither a confirmation nor a rejection; rather, it is a cryptic and incongruent response which basically states: "I don't notice you, you are not here, you don't exist."

In our work with families, we have discovered another method of disconfirmation even more deadly and subtle: *it is the very author of the message who qualifies himself as nonexistant,* expressing in some way, "I'm not really here, I don't exist in the relationship with you."

The frequency and importance of this maneuver was first brought to our attention during a session with the family of a preadolescent psychotic, who unexpectedly came out with "I am trying hard to have my mother materialize." Only in that moment did we realize the meaning of the vague impression created by the mother that she was an outsider, bored with what was going on, and in no way *involved* in what was happening. In communicating this to us, she provoked that sense of futility and exhaustion, which until that point we had generally attributed to the "type" of family transaction.

How was it possible to reach someone who was not there? And inversely, how could we exist in a relationship with someone who did not exist (like the "little man upon the stair" in the nursery rhyme)?[3] From then on, we began to notice the frequency of this maneuver of autodisconfirmation resulting in disconfirmation of others in the family in schizophrenic transaction.

When the couple turns to therapy, the game is already crystallized, and the therapists must deal with a symmetry hidden behind an accumulation of maneuvers so complex and confusing as to even make the couple appear affectionate and devoted, each concerned with the other's well-being. Whatever the case, affectionate or not, it is clear that the two are in fact inseparable, and we are tempted to ask ourselves, "What on earth can keep them together in such a difficult relationship?"

It has often been stated by students of the family in schizophrenic transaction that the parents in these families have fragile personalities, that they cling to their partner in the constant fear of abandonment as well as of true intimacy. Our own experience with these families has made us understand that such a belief, which initially we had shared, had seriously held back our work and had led us to commit errors which were sometimes irreparable.

This erroneous belief led us to consider the feelings shown in the session as a "reality." When we saw a family member in a happy or depressed mood, we would conclude: "He *is* happy"; or "He *is* depressed, I wonder why."

We had also been conditioned by the linguistic model, according to which the predicate we link to the subject becomes an inherent quality of that subject while, in effect, it is no more than a function of the relationship. For example, if a patient appeared to be sad, we concluded he *was* sad, and we went so far as to try to understand *why* he was sad, inviting and encouraging him to speak to us about his sadness.

Once we had gone from the individual to the systemic model, it was, and still is, difficult to free ourselves from this linguistic conditioning, and to put into practice our new understanding: appearance is not necessarily reality.

In order to bracket the sentiments, in the sense of intrapsychic reality, we had to force ourselves to systematical-ly substitute the verb *to seem* for the verb *to be*. Thus, if Mr. Bianchi *seemed* sad during a session, we had to make an effort to avoid thinking that he *was* sad (this being undecidable) and therefore not to be interested in finding out why.

For example, if, during a heated argument between her husband and her son, Mrs. Rossi seemed bored and faraway, it was a mistake to conclude that she really was bored, and to discuss and try to discover the reason for that boredom. Instead, we found it more productive to silently observe the effects of her behavior on the others in the group, ourselves included. Here again, it was easy to fall into the habits of observation imposed upon us by the linguistic model.

This step, elementary in theory but extremely difficult in practical application, led us to our first effective therapeutic intervention in nonschizophrenic families and became a basic tool in our approach to the family in schizophrenic transaction. With this we had to force upon ourselves this linguistic deconditioning by the further substitution of the verb *to show* in our team discussion. For example: Mr. Rossi *shows us* in the session a subtle erotic interest in his daughter.

In the first phase of our work, when confronted with such behavior, we concluded: this father is incestuously attached to his daughter. As a result, we tried to clarify and bring out the issue, but only succeeded in stimulating denials, disqualifications, and the eventual discontinuation of therapy.

It was these very errors and their instructive feedbacks which led us to act as if all behaviors and attitudes of the family in schizophrenic transaction were mere *moves* whose sole purpose were to perpetuate the family game, as if everything were only exhibited, were only "pseudo."

Once again, it became clear how the use of the verb *to be* condemns us to think according to the linear model, to make arbitrary punctuation, to inquire on the reality of undecidables, and to postulate that a causality exists, thus losing ourselves in an intricacy of endless explanations and hypotheses.

In the following record of a family session, we can see how the substitution of the verb *to show* for the verb *to be* clarifies the family game:

The father, Mr. Franchi, shows, during the session, a veiled erotic interest in the designated patient, who, for her part, shows hostility and scorn toward him. Mrs. Franchi shows an intense jealousy toward husband and daughter, while she shows a strong affection toward her other daughter, who, in turn, shows no sign of reciprocating this affection.

This new way of describing the essentials of what is going on in the system was and still remains a major step, for the game immediately stands out clearly. Each of the parents threatens the other with the move of a rival (usually an internal member of the group).[4] The presumed rivals, for their part, carry out countermoves which are essential to the game, whose continuation is assured by ambiguity: they can be neither allies nor adversaries, neither winners nor losers, or the game will end.

In fact, if the designated patient were to show a return of love toward her father instead of scorn and hostility, the alliance between the two would be clearly stated. The display of this alliance would constrain the other daughter to openly ally herself with her mother, showing a return of affection and love. In this case, the symmetry would be open, and the struggle between the two factions declared. But, it is necessary that the homeostasis of the group be preserved in order to insure the perpetuation of the game. The schizophrenic game and homeostasis are, in fact, synonymous, just as ambiguity and feints are essential to the status quo.

At this point, we must ask ourselves, What is the real danger threatening the family in schizophrenic transaction? What is the fear that drives all the members of the group to behave as described above? Perhaps the fear of losing the others as persons, of finding themselves alone and without support in a world perceived as hostile and dangerous? But, we must ask ourselves, *are* they afraid of these things or are they only *showing* us they are afraid of these things?

The fear comes from another source: it comes from hubris, not as a predicate in the traditional sense (that is, a psychic quality inherent to an individual) but in the sense of a function in this type of relationship where symmetry increases hubris and hubris symmetry. For this reason, the game must not end. Everyone hopes that one day he will make it. The essential thing is that the whole team remain on the field. The state of alarm is always urgent: any withdrawal by one of the players is sensed as a great danger. Will the game be able to go on? Everything is geared to its continuation, and any means is valid if it can hold the players, incite and stimulate them to greater involvement.

The repertoire of moves is infinite and one rule of the game is: anything goes. Eroticism, incest, infidelity, hostility, affectionate indulgence, dependence, independence, boredom (with the game), interest (elsewhere), etc., etc. This endless variety of moves is admirably aided by the so-called thinking disorders, which are so useful in creating a smokescreen for the observer, and which skillfully render metacommunication, any solving of the riddle, and any clarification of issues impossible.

Our first suspicion of the existence of such a barrier of moves and maneuvers was prompted by repeated observation of certain fixed patterns of interaction in the parents of schizophrenic adolescents.

Very often the two partners use maneuvers which are apparently opposed. The one shows himself as being a potential fugitive from the relationship: he is uninhibited, anticonformist, unafraid of new experiences, and ready to start a new life if necessary. He is full of interests and has many friends and possibilities, although in his present situation he is worn out, exhausted, and at the end of his rope. The other member of the couple, always with a thousand contradictions, shows himself as being the stable partner, ready to renounce all in his dedication to the marriage, profoundly in love,[5] and incapable of sustaining the loss of his spouse.

The observer could easily be induced to believe that the fugitive partner is really the more autonomous of the two, and that he really has the intention of leaving. But also here, the "intention" is a mere move. His threat has the result of nailing his partner to the playing board, and influences the other members of the group to behave in such a way as to prevent his escape. In this way the circle tightens and the "fugitive" is forced to remain.

The two partners, the "fugitive" as well as the "stable," are equally inseparable. They are accomplices in the same game, united by the same fear: that of losing the other as a partner in the game.

Our work with the couple in schizophrenic transaction has brought us to the fundamental hypothesis that the mistaken epistemology of such a couple, beyond what it shows, is hubris, that is, the hidden presumption which each one holds: that he will sooner or later be able to gain unilateral control of the definition of the relationship.

The presumption is obviously mistaken since it is based on a mistaken epistemology inherent to linear linguistic conditioning. *No one* can have linear control in an interaction which is, by definition, circular. If the partner does not accept that his position in the relationship is defined as complementary, he can always signal to the other through communicational metalevels that the other's superiority is not really superiority.

In order to clarify this concept, we can refer to an example in ethology. In a fight between two wolves, the weaker signals his surrender by rolling over on his back, presenting his undefended throat to his opponent. The victor accepts this sign of defeat, abandoning his aggressive behavior.[6] Thus, the transaction between the two wolves ends without ambiguity: there is clearly a winner and a loser, and the pack regulates itself according to this conclusion.

We can imagine what would happen to the wolf species if the loser returned to signal to the winner (as usually happens with a couple in schizophrenic transaction) that he has not *really* won, since the winner has interpreted certain signs as meaning surrender when they did not *really* mean that at all. (We have to try again . . . maybe if we try again . . . who knows?) In fact, the sine qua non of the schizophrenic play, which is exclusively human, is that there should never be a real winner or loser, according to the positions in the relationship which are always either pseudocomplementary or pseudosymmetrical.

A game of this type can therefore have no conclusion, since the result will always be undecidable: the winner has perhaps lost, the loser has perhaps won and so on; the challenge is always there. Each one endeavors to constantly provoke his adversary with a series of tactics which become more and more refined with experience.

The skillful combination of depression and exhaustion: "I feel worn out, unloved; do something to liven up the game."

The air of boredom and of being faraway: "Do you think you can reach me? I am somewhere else."

The desperate appeal for help with the concluding message: "What a pity! I wanted you to help me so much, but you couldn't do it even this time. Oh well, try it again, maybe the next time. . . ."

These are only a few of the thousand tactics used in the schizophrenic game of "Now you win, now you don't."

In the context of what we have said earlier in this chapter, the double bind, first described by Bateson and his collaborators as occurring with maximum frequency in families in schizophrenic transaction, can be considered a communicational mode suited to transmitting and maintaining a challenge which presents no way out and no possible end. Such a communicational mode can be summed up in the following way: on the verbal level an injunction is made which, on a second level (usually nonverbal), is disqualified. At the same time, another message is given that it is forbidden to make comments, that is, to metacommunicate on the incongruence of the two levels, and that it is forbidden to leave the field.

Such a move obviously does not allow the person who receives the injunction to adopt a complementary position (through obedience to the injunction), since it is not clear what he has to obey.

At the same time, he may not place himself in a symmetrical position, that is, in a position of disobeying, since, once again, it is impossible to make out which is the real injunction to rebel against. In our opinion, both the prohibition against metacommunicating and the prohibition against leaving the field are already implicit in the impossibility of assuming a definable position in the interaction. In fact, only a well-defined position can permit metacommunication or the abandonment of the field, that is, the redefinition of the relation; *it is possible to redefine a relationship only when that relationship has been previously clearly defined.*

In the situation of double bind, however, the recipient is obliged to keep himself permanently on guard and in a state of alarm until he can find a third response which avoids both the symmetrical and complementary positions. He has no other choice but posing to the adversary an identical puzzle.

In a more recent publication of Bateson's, "The Cybernetics of Self: A Theory of Alcoholism" (1972), we have found many points pertinent to our own study of families in schizophrenic transaction. In this paper, much of which is based on the position toward alcoholism taken by Alcoholics Anonymous, Bateson demonstrates how the first step of the alcoholic toward his own cure consists of his definitive and unequivocal recognition of himself as powerless in the face of his adversary: the bottle.

It seems to us that the alcoholic has transferred to the bottle the provocatory challenge always present in his transactional system, which is in some way similar to the one we found in our families in schizophrenic transaction. The challenge is hubris, the pride to succeed, one day or another, to be stronger than the bottle, to be able to defeat it by being able to take only a sip, without needing to drain the glass.[7]

But here also, exactly as in his system, the alcoholic finds himself, no matter what he does, in a double bind: if he does not drink, has he really won? Or rather, has he lost because he has avoided the provocation? He should therefore try again in order to convince himself that "he can." But if he goes on a binge, has he really lost? Or rather has he won because he has challenged the bottle without dying? Basically, he could have not drunk, or drunk more....

How does the alcoholic, in his contact with A.A., come to accept a definitive complementary position vis 'a vis the bottle? According to Bateson, the philosophy of A.A. is that an alcoholic can be helped *only* when he has hit the very bottom, and has been reduced to the point of asking for help. Only then can he accept the humiliating sentence of A.A.: once an alcoholic, always an alcoholic.

If he has not yet arrived at the point at which he can accept such a definition, he returns to his symmetric position with the bottle, drinking and holding back, challenging and surrendering, playing with death until he is forced to admit defeat and comes back for help.

In this insistence that the alcoholic touch the bottom before coming for help, and therefore in the explicit prescription that he do so, we can recognize the essential thrust used by A.A. to change the alcoholic. This time it is against A.A. that the alcoholic has to measure himself *in order to demonstrate the falseness of the humiliating sentence.* In order to succeed he has only one choice: he will no longer be an alcoholic. He thus becomes symmetric in regard to the clear definition A.A. has given of him: Once an alcoholic, always an alcoholic. He accepts the complementary position in relation to the bottle in order to be symmetric with the definition (to reject it).

The therapeutic paradox consists of having forced the alcoholic to adopt the following position: "To show you (A.A.) that you are wrong, that is, that I won't always be an alcoholic like you say, I don't care any more about the bottle. We can even say it's stronger than I am, that doesn't matter. The important thing is that I show you that I am not what you say I am: always an alcoholic."

The game with A.A. has become far more interesting than that with the bottle, especially because those who attempt to give this definitive label to the alcoholic call themselves ex-alcoholics, thus paradoxically denying the finality of the sentence.

How can we respond, therefore, to the question posed by Bateson at the end of his paper: "Is complementarity *always* somehow better than symmetry?" We agreed with Bateson that a symmetrical behavior by the individual in regard to the great system which transcends him, is certainly an error. But, in the relationship between individuals, there can be no question of better or worse between symmetry or complementarity, because they are functions inherent to the relationship. What is essential for an interpersonal relationship not to be psychotic, is the unequivocal clarity of its definition—precisely what is forbidden, as we have seen, in schizophrenic interaction.

chapter 4

THE IDENTIFIED PATIENT

How can we explain the behavior, commonly designated schizophrenic, that takes place in the evolutionary history of that peculiar paradoxical game characterizing the family in schizophrenic transaction?

It is neither more nor less than one of the many moves used by one of the members of the group, a move whose pragmatic effect is a further reinforcement of the game.

It is a paradoxical game, absolutely unique. It is a competition similar to a bizarre poker game in which each player, determined to win at any cost, limits himself to observing the motions and expressions of the others, while remaining restrained by the shared and unspoken prohibition against placing the cards on the table once and for all.

It is an absurd game, whose players are determined to prevail while remaining within a game whose principal rule precisely forbids either prevailing or, reciprocally, succumbing. Moreover, it is a game which permits and even encourages each player (in turn, so that no one has to give up) to *believe* he is winning, as long as he does so in secret.

It is an interminable game, since each partner, led on by hubris—"As long as I keep playing I have a chance of winning"—is compelled by an extreme tension to try and try again.

It is a competition similar to that which takes place between the alcoholic and the bottle, but with a substantial difference:

the bottle is an object, it is always there, and cannot make the countermove or leave the field. The alcoholic can always restate the challenge and start all over again, while the bottle stays fixed and immobile. It cannot seem bored or exasperated with the game, and, most important of all, it cannot make the threat that it wants to stop, that it wants to change the game.

Between living beings, however, the transaction is circular. Each can respond to a challenge with another challenge, to a move with a countermove. One can clearly show that he is fed up, sick and tired, that the *others* are not doing all they can, and that he is *going* to get out. This threat, all the more credible because of the common fear that the game will end, can in extreme cases be so credible as to provoke one of the adversaries to an even more powerful move: that of communicating that the relationship has become untenable to the point that he has in fact *already withdrawn from it.* Although still physically present, he is already *different, alienated, estranged.*

This metamorphosis[8] of one member of the group conveys the message, The relationship is no longer tenable, the change is necessary.

But who has to change? The *others* of course! But which change should they make? It is so simple: *They should not be what they are!*

In other words, it is as if the identified patient were saying: "Only if you were not what you are can I be what I am not but what I should have been. To help me you don't have to do anything, it wouldn't help anyway. In order to really help me, you should really *be* what you should have been."

Thus we can formulate the schizophrenic message: "It's not that you should *do* something different; you should *be* different. Only in this way can you help me to be what I'm not, but what I could be if you were not what you are."

Here we are confronted with the genius of the schizophrenic—who has become a master of the acrobatic leap from one logical level to another, who changes the logical level while signaling that he is not really changing it, who, like a Christ,[9] has made the ultimate, supreme leap from the class of *doing* to the class of all classes, that of *being.*

The schizophrenic message, therefore, brings the paradox to the extreme, with the impossible made absolute through the substitution of the verb *to be* for the verb *to do*. Let's go back for the moment to see how the schizophrenic first learned to manipulate and confound the categories of doing and the categories of being.

As Haley has observed, in families in schizophrenic transaction, not only does each member find himself continually dealing with conflictual levels in the messages he receives, but he finds also that his responses are always classified as "wrong," or better yet, as "not exactly right."

Thus, if a member of the family says something, there is always another member ready to make him understand that he didn't say it quite as he should have, that he should have said it differently. If he tries to help someone else, he receives the message that he doesn't do it often enough, or well enough—in other words, that he has been of no help at all. If he makes a proposal, someone else immediately shows doubts about his right to make proposals. At the same time, if he makes no proposals, he is made to understand that he really has no right to depend on the others' decisions.

Everyone, in other words, has always felt that he has never quite done the right thing, *without its ever being said explicitly what it is he should do to do the right thing*.

Now we can understand how a person in such a learning context, where leaving the field is unthinkable, finds a definitive move in the superparadox: "It's not that you don't *do* what you should do; it's that you're not as you should *be*" (where "as you should be" obviously remains as vague and undefined as "what you should do").

From General Systems Theory and cybernetics, we know that the autocorrective mechanism maintaining the homeostasis of the system is that of negative feedback; schizophrenic behavior appears to be an extremely powerful negative feedback, all the more because it is paradoxical. When one of the members of the family makes a too credible move indicating that he intends to do something different, he receives as a countermove the even more credible response: "ahem . . . I am already different, but this doesn't depend on my will; maybe I am possessed by something mysterious which makes me different. I can't do anything about it. But perhaps I'm different because you aren't different, but if you tried to be different. . . ." Such a message, such an invocation for change on the part of the *schizophrenic behavior* is so credible that it can convince everyone of its reality. But how can we *know* whether the person presenting such a schizophrenic behavior is or is not invoking a change?

In the systemic epistemology, this is undecidable. Any pronouncement on "reality" or "non-reality" is an illusion of alternatives. All we can observe and verify is a pragmatic effect: someone shows that he is invoking a change; the result of this message is the absence of change.

It is said in the literature on this subject that in rigidly controlled systems such as families presenting a schizophrenic member, every change is felt as a threat. Here we are dealing with solicitations for change which are made to the family from the outside (social, political, or cultural solicitations) as well as from the inside (birth, the death or departure of a member, the adolescent crisis of a child, etc.). To such changes the system reacts negatively, with further rigidity.

Our own learning through trials and errors with these families has led us to conclude that even real and concrete changes, whether introduced from the outside or from the inside, are absorbed in the ongoing family game. They thus become further threats to the continuation of the game and thereby pragmatically strengthen it.

In two families treated in our institute, the intensification of the chronic and latent threat of total breakdown of both parents (made even more credible, in one of the cases, by the physical collapse of an "exhausted" mother) coincided with the engagement of one of the sons. It became necessary for the families to redistribute the roles in the game, to form new coalitions, and to carry out countermoves of various types to guarantee the continuation of the game. The loyalty of the various members (to the game) functioned, in these two families, to the point of rendering necessary the appearance of schizophrenic behavior in one of the children.

We can observe similar results in the cases of other families with a child in adolescent crisis. If an adolescent change takes place, or better yet, if it is in some way permitted, the system immediately puts itself in action to reorganize the game according to the new situation. In some cases, a second child will exhibit all the signs of "the crazy teenager," thus insuring the continuation of the game ad infinitum.[10]

From this perspective, we consider as moves in the game even certain typical behaviors of the adolescent crisis which appear in the member who will later present a schizophrenic behavior.

It is often said, following the punctuation of the linear model, that the parents of the patient have stubbornly opposed themselves to his autonomy, and that the patient, for his part, has had great difficulty in becoming autonomous because he has assumed an archaic superego which has forbidden his autonomy. If, working with the family, we adopt the circular and systemic epistemology, we can observe that what *everyone* obeys are the rules of the game, and that the game perpetuates itself through threats and counterthreats, among which one of the most powerful is that one of the participants will withdraw and leave the field.

In a group in which everything manifested is meant to maintain the game and its perpetuations, even the move of adolescent autonomy will elicit the foreseen pragmatic effect of closing ranks, that is, negative feedbacks of every type which will forbid the adolescent to go ahead.

When these negative feedbacks occur, we see the adolescent reacting with psychotic behavior. If the therapist naively advises the parents to give the teenager some leeway, not to oppress him, and to try to valorize in his behavior the positive aspects of his adolescent protest, we immediately see the family united in total disqualification. The parents, depressed and hostile, say that they have never overprotected the child, but that they have followed the advice regardless and achieved no results. And we see the adolescent ready to reopen the game with the therapist: "Anyway, it's too late. A mysterious anguish has taken hold of me. I really want to but I can't do anything."

From a strictly circular and systemic perspective any punctuation in the sense of before and after, cause and effect, can only be arbitrary. To explain this we can refer to the case of a family of three.

During the same period in which Gianni, the son, began to show signs of adolescent change, the father had a serious setback in his business. Irritable, without appetite and showing loss of weight, he manifested signs of depression. The mother, who had years before cut off relations with her family because of their disapproval of her marriage, effected a reconciliation. She began to see her mother and sister frequently, and showed herself to be much consoled by these visits, which often were extended to overnight stays. She began to repeat certain criticisms of her husband made by her sister, who, recently divorced, appeared rejuvenated and full of wordly initiative. Toward Gianni, the mother changed her attitude: she showed herself to be less interested, distracted, and slightly bored. She spent a good deal of time on the phone, but if her husband or Gianni were to "surprise" her, she would rapidly hang up.

After several months of these goings-on, Gianni began to show signs of psychotic behavior. His mother confined herself to the house to dedicate herself exclusively to him. The father, also worried about Gianni, had improved in his health and was able to return to his work: "I have to work hard to pay the large bills incurred by Gianni's illness!"

We may be tempted to ask who carried out the first move in the game. Gianni, who threatened his mother with hints of an adolescent change: "If you abandon me for your family, I will abandon you"? The mother, who threatened her husband with her rediscovery of a family she believed to have been right in disapproving her marriage to a man of so little worth? Who threatened Gianni with her newfound consolation in these reestablished affectionate family relationships, with her sudden disinterest in him? The father, who threatened his wife and his son with his demonstration of being on the verge of breakdown and bankruptcy: "If you abandon me, you will destroy me, and you will have to take the consequences"?

With difficulty and by gradual steps, through innumerable errors and disappointments, we came to understand that to understand the game we had to force ourselves to observe all appearances in these families as merely the pragmatic effect of moves each in their turn soliciting countermoves[11] in the service of the game and its perpetuation.

As we were slowly able to force ourselves to consider as mere moves hostility, tenderness, coldness, depression, weakness, efficiency, anguish, stolidity, confusion, requests for help, etc., we also became able to regard the identified patient's invocation for change as simply the most striking move in the game, so credible that it almost seems "reality."

It is a powerful paradox, which offers no way of escape and which traps all the members of the family.

The author of the move, the identified patient, finds himself as trapped as the others in the mistaken epistemology of the linear model: the false belief that *he* dominates the system and has power over it. But he is just another one of the slaves of the game, who is insuring its continuation with the opening of a new paradoxical escalation toward linear pseudo-power. To be precise, a new escalation begins between the pseudo-power of the schizophrenic and the pseudo-power of those who declare themselves guilty or responsible for his condition. Who has more power in the effort to define the relationship defined as undefinable? The schizophrenic? Or whoever has made him such?

For the discovery that this declaration of guilt is but another move aiding the hidden escalation of force in the system, we are particularly indebted to the families with psychotic children.

These children didn't show very much gratitude when we told them how sensitive and generous they were for putting themselves at the disposition of what they supposed to be their families' needs, without their even being asked to do so. In fact one of these children, six years old, responded to this "praise" by leaping upon one of the therapists and scratching his face. Another child, seven years old, let loose with a kick that left its sign for many a day afterwards. It should be noted that these children had never presented violent behavior during previous sessions.

Since these children were unaware of the circular nature of the game, they erroneously believed themselves to be the initiators of the rules, and to have unidirectional power over the system. In this, they were influenced by the attitude of the other members of the system, who declared themselves impotent in the face of such psychotic power, but who at the same time restimulated the escalation toward pseudo-power by defining themselves as in some way responsible for the psychosis. We could observe on several occasions how the declarations of guilt made by the mothers of psychotic children (I never accepted him . . . I wasn't mature enough . . . I couldn't stand him . . . *I should be different . . . I should accept and love him*), declarations encouraged by the erroneous causal epistemology of most psychiatrists and psychologists, are no more than symmetric moves in the service of the perpetuation of the schizophrenic game, and of the tireless hidden symmetry between the members of the group.

Moreover, we were able to remark an astonishing phenomenon: *none* of our mothers of psychotic children has ever been willing to accept our calm statement that her child was the victim of no one, that spontaneously, without having been asked to do so, he had generously assumed the burden of sacrificing himself in order to help the others in what he *presumed* to be their profound needs.[12] The mother immediately disqualifies any such statement, attempting to reconquer her symmetric position (in respect both to the therapist and to her child) by redefining herself as a "guilty" mother.

Such feedbacks aroused in us at first a feeling of embarassment. We had naively expected some sort of expression of gratitude and relief, and instead we found ourselves once again confronted with our own shortsightedness and lack of systemic vision. What about the father, where did he fit in? And what about the hidden and exasperated symmetry of the couple, since between an "absent" father and an "overprotective and pathogenic" mother there is always a way to pass the accusations back and forth to perpetuate the escalation to the undecidable?

Thus, between mistaken convictions of power and mistaken convictions of guilt, everyone remains in the game, serving it as both victim and accomplice. If he is temporarily placed in an institution, the "schizophrenic" will still remain at the disposition of the game, the moves and countermoves being carried out through the skillful manipulation of visits, discharges, and readmissions. Sometimes the game can be successfully restored to its prepsychotic state. If this doesn't work out, the family in the long run can adjust the game to the patient's absence, relegating him forever to some institution. But, at this point, in the extreme exasperation of hubris, the game has become for the patient his very existence. He believes himself to have made the last move, to be in the position of power: he is the one who calls for change, but *can be changed by no one*.

If, instead of the traditional mental institution, the patient is placed in a therapeutic community which is generous, open-minded, and eager to change him, we see the same game beginning all over again, in which symmetry stimulates hubris, and hubris symmetry. The deeply rooted symmetric premise we find in all men is also deeply rooted in those who wish to change the patient. Who has more power in defining a relationship defined as undefinable? The schizophrenic? Or those who believe they can change him to the point of feeling guilty if they don't succeed in doing so? Or those who don't help those who believe they can change him? etc. etc.

Thus, in the paradoxical escalation between false beliefs of power and false beliefs of guilt we can reconstruct the parameters, rules, communicational modes, denied coalitions, and secret battles which tacitly reorganize the original family game.

If instead the patient enters individual therapy and the therapist is eager to change him and lets that attitude be seen, we see the patient seducing the therapist little by little into the symmetric game.[13] The patient will be saying to him, in his own special way of saying things, that is, cryptic, confused, and covert: "I would like to change, but I can't, because you don't *really* help me to change; to really help me change, you should be what someone else should have been, but was not. You've let me down, I was really counting on you. Why don't you try again? Please don't give up. Try again to be exactly what someone else should have been but was not. Only in that way could I be...etc., etc."

As can clearly be seen, it is not easy for a person to extricate himself from this game once he has had the misfortune to get into it.[14]

Part III

explore

chapter 5

THERAPEUTIC INTERVENTIONS:
A LEARNING PROCESS THROUGH
TRIAL AND ERROR

Therapeutic interventions in the family, as we have gradually devised, applied, and critically examined them, appear to be, at a certain point, no more than a learning process acquired by the therapists through trial and error. We will see, in fact, in the following and in numerous examples that will be given later, how errors are no less than an essential component of that learning process which is therapy of the family. In fact, since any learning superior to zero learning (Bateson 1972, pp. 279-308) proceeds through trial and error, both trial and error are indispensable to produce, through feedbacks, more and more information.

Let us consider a relatively simple experimental learning situation such as that of a rat placed in a maze. In order to arrive at the cell containing a feeding tray, he will initiate a series of explanatory moves, in which he will come across many obstacles, dead ends, runs made impassable by painful electric shocks, etc. From these trials and errors, the rat will obtain a series of bits of information which will lead him to operate a progressive revision of his choices among the unchangeable set of alternatives. Theoretically, the rat will arrive the more quickly at this goal (the feeding tray) if he takes into account the information coming from the errors he has made, and, inversely, will arrive more slowly, or not at all, if he does not. In this sense, therefore, an error is not really an error, but becomes part and parcel of the trial. The real error, in the sense in which we usually use the word, occurs only when the obtained information is *not* taken into consideration, and therefore there is no change in behavior. This persistence in the error annuls any possibility of learning. It is clear that the experimental rat will very seldom arrive at the feeding tray at his first trial.

If we apply this example to the therapeutic situation, we can see that even the therapists, when they have entered the family labyrinth, are rarely able to provoke and gather, at the first, a sufficient number of feedbacks to reveal a nodal point, dissolving which, with a minimum of energy, they can obtain the maximum amount of change.

The greatest difficulty, as one can imagine, is found in the case of the family in schizophrenic transaction. Here we find ourselves in a labyrinth even more complex than the mythical one of Knossos. We should not forget that the family in schizophrenic transaction gives us information which is intended to confuse us at every turn, and everything it shows proves to be a trap. Thus, we find ourselves, like Theseus but without the silken thread of Ariadne, facing an incredibly intricate series of passages with heavy gates clanging shut behind us, blind alleys, mysterious caverns, and splendid and inviting doorways. Here, to find our way out, we must learn many things, keep up our courage, and remember the errors we have made. We learn, for example, that certain inviting doorways, clearly visible and marked by the passage of our predecessors who had trustingly entered them, are traps: those who enter them risk falling into an abyss without exit. Other insignificant and well-hidden doorways, or passages that can be entered only on hands and knees, lead to the cell of the Minotaur. It is necessary, in this labyrinth, to move always with caution, to develop an acute sensitivity to feedbacks, to resist the temptation of persisting in the same errors, to be free of arrogance, and to be constantly aware of the ever present dangers. Above all, we must realize that, even though we may be in a hurry, we must allow ourselves enough time to provoke illuminating feedbacks.

We must keep in mind that the set of alternatives does not remain invariable, as in the elementary metaphor of the rat, but is continually changing; the only stable points are the redundancies which occur during the therapeutic session.

For example, we not infrequently observe in the couple in schizophrenic transaction a striking variation of mood in one member or the other, from session to session. The redundancy of the phenomenon, however, is that if one spouse appears to be upset or depressed, the other appears relaxed and positive. We can also observe how, in certain families, the disqualification or sidetracking of the therapists is a constant, even if it will not always fall to the same member to accomplish this goal.

Another clear example of redundancy can be seen in the case of one of our families which showed, from session to session, a great inventiveness in confusing both the issue and the therapists. Every time the discussion was brought to the subject of the maternal grandmother, we observed a drastic lowering of the group I.Q.!

The theoreticians of the system have spoken of p_s, as being that nodal point in which converge the greatest number of functions essential to the maintenance of a system. Therefore, if one directs an intervention toward the nodal point p_s, one will get maximum change of the system with a minimum expense of energy.

Working within a certain period of time, over long intervals and with attention always centered on the feedbacks of the family, one has the sensation of proceeding by layers, almost in a circular manner, from the outermost points toward the central nodal point, action upon which can trigger the greatest transformation. This fact has permitted Rabkin (1972) to declare with great acumen: "Instead of a difficult mechanistic approach (which necessarily involves a great expense of energy) there will develop a new profession within the General Systems Theory which will make things take place by transformation, rather than by hard work." He adds that transformations are changes which should be triggered suddenly and concludes with the pleasantly humorous observation that the Protestant ethic, based upon hard work, thrift, and individualism, seems the exact antithesis of the systemic ethic.

After this premise, we can begin to analyze the first difficulty encountered in our journey into the labyrinth of the system of the family in schizophrenic transaction.

chapter 6

THE TYRANNY OF LINGUISTIC CONDITIONING

A series of disappointing experiences in the psychotherapeutic treatment of families in schizophrenic transaction forced us to realize that the greatest obstacle confronting us in our approach to the family, and above all to the family in schizophrenic transaction, is within us. This obstacle is our own, and inevitable, linguistic conditioning.

We should clarify immediately that we are particularly indebted for this realization to two fundamental works: Gregory Bateson's *Steps to an Ecology of Mind* (1972) and Harley Shands's *The War with Words* (1971). These works stimulated us to make the effort, by no means small, to change our linear and causal epistemology to a more correct one which would permit us the invention of more adequate therapeutic methods.

The observation and the detailed classification of the communicational disturbances peculiar to the family in schizophrenic transaction certainly represent a conquest in the field of scientific research. For us, however, they represented a source of error as long as we sought to introduce change in the family through the correction of such communicational peculiarities: correction which we based upon pointing out such peculiarities and encouraging the reformulation of messages in the "correct" way. In other words, we tried to "teach" the family to communicate functionally. We also believed we could fruitfully use the verbal code, mistakenly presuming it to be shared by the family in schizophrenic transaction.

Finally we were able to realize how much our belonging to a verbal world conditions us. In fact, since rational thought is formed through language, we conceptualize reality (whatever that may be) according to the linguistic model which thus becomes for us the same thing as reality.

But language is not reality. In fact, the former is linear while the latter is living and circular. Shands says that

> language prescribes for us a linear ordering of data in discursive sequence. Overwhelmingly and unconsciously influenced by linguistic method, we then decide and enforce acceptance of the notion that the universe is organized on a linear basis, in cause and effect patterns of general relevance. Since language demands subject and predicate, actor and acted upon, in many different combinations and permutations, we conclude that this is the structure of the world. But we soon learn, in any delicate and complicated context, that we cannot find such a concretely defined order except by imposing it, and we thereafter operate by setting a limit in the middle of a continuous variation which makes the distinction between "hypo-" and "hyper-," between "normal" and "abnormal," between "black" and "white." [1971, p. 32]

All the same, we are imprisoned by the absolute incompatibility between the two primary systems in which the human being lives: the living system, dynamic and circular, and the symbolic system (language), descriptive, static, and linear.

In developing his species-specific characteristic, language, which is also the tool of tools for the organization and transmission of culture, man has to integrate two entirely different communicational modes: the analogical and the digital. Since language is descriptive and linear, we are forced, in order to describe a transaction, to use a dichotomization or to introduce a series of dichotomizations. The dichotomization which we are forced to use by the very nature of language, requiring a "before" and "after," a subject and object (in the sense of he who *performs* the action and he who *receives* the action), implies a postulate of cause and effect, and, in consequence, a moralistic definition.

Moralism is intrinsic to language because the linguistic model is linear. For example, as we shall see in chapter 15, when confronted by an identified patient, a young woman who played the role of a rough and violent ancestral father, one could be tempted to postulate, as cause of the "pathology," the inefficiency and passivity of the real father, thus slipping into a moralistic judgment of him. In the circular model, however, the two behaviors can be considered simply complementary functions of the same game.

In the case of the family in schizophrenic transaction, where the two communicational levels, the analogic and the digital, are in competition, our linguistic conditioning led us to a series of errors, the most significant of which can be summarized:

a. conceptualization of the living reality of the family in a linear sense rather than in a systemic-circular sense
b. judgment of the communicational modes of the family as "mistaken" in comparison to our own, and the consequent attempt to correct them
c. our basing ourselves almost exclusively on the digital code, that is, on the level of the content of the message, in the attempt to act therapeutically

The change of direction, epistemological and methodological, that we have sought to carry out will become more clear through the exposition and analysis of the therapeutic interventions to be described in the following chapters. These therapeutic interventions are characterized by the common effort to overcome the linguistic barrier in order to enter the world of circularity.

chapter 7

POSITIVE CONNOTATION

The basic therapeutic principle which we call *positive connotation* was initially inspired by our need not to contradict ourselves when giving a paradoxical prescription of the symptom to the identified patient. How, after all, can one prescribe a behavior one has just criticized?

But, if *not* negatively connoting the symptom of the identified patient was easy, we could not say the same about all the behaviors of the other members, especially of the parents, which often appear correlated to that symptom. This traditional view easily leads to the temptation to use an arbitrary punctuation: correlating the symptom to the symptomatic behaviors of the "others," according to a causal connection. Thus it happened, not infrequently, that we found ourselves indignant and angry with the parents of the patient. Such was the tyranny of the linguistic model; such was our difficulty in freeing ourselves of it. We had to force ourselves to fully realize the antitherapeutic consequences of such a mistaken epistemology.

In fact, making a positive connotation of the symptom of the identified patient and a negative connotation of the symptomatic behavior of the others, is the same as drawing a dividing line between the members of the family system, arbitrarily defining some as "good" and others as "bad," and thereby precluding for the therapists any access to the family as a systemic unity.

It thus became clear that access to the systemic model was possible only if we were to make a positive connotation of _both_ the symptom of the identified patient and the symptomatic behaviors of the others, saying, for example, that all the observable behaviors of the group as a whole appeared to be inspired by the common goal of preserving the cohesion of the family group. In this way, the therapists were able to put _all_ the members of the group on the same level, thus avoiding involvement in any alliances or divisions into subgroups, which are the daily bread of such systems' malfunction. Dysfunctional families are in fact regularly, especially in moments of crisis, prone to such divisions and factional battles, which are characterized by the distribution of such stereotyped labels as "bad," "sick," "weak," "inefficient," "carrier of hereditary or social taints," etc.

Therefore the primary function of the positive connotation of all the observable behaviors of the group is that of permitting the therapists access to the systemic model. 15

But, one may ask, why must the connotation be positive, that is, a confirmation? Can't the same results be obtained through a global negative connotation (rejection)? One could say, for example, that both the symptom of the identified patient and the symptomatic behaviors of the family are "wrong," since they both attempt to maintain the stability of a "wrong" system—"wrong" because it generates pain and suffering. In doing so, however, one would be implying that the "wrong" system should change. And here, we should point out that every living system has three fundamental characteristics: (1) _totality_ (the system is largely independent of the elements which make it up); (2) _autocorrective capacity_ (and therefore the tendency toward homeostasis); (3) _capacity for transformation._

By implying with a negative judgment that the system should change, one rejects that system, in that it is characterized by a prevalent homeostatic tendency. In doing so, one precludes any possibility of being accepted by dysfunctional groups, which are _always_ characterized by this tendency. In addition, one would be committing the theoretical error of drawing an arbitrary dividing line between two of the equally functional characteristics in every living system—the homeostatic tendency and the capacity for transformation—as if the two were opposites, the former "bad" and the latter "good."

In every living system neither the homeostatic tendency nor the capacity for transformation can be judged good or bad, better or worse; each is a functional characteristic of the system, neither of which can exist without the other. Their combination occurs circularly, according to a continuum, substituting for the linear model of *either/or,* the circular model of *more or less.*

All the same, as Shands points out, man tirelessly pursues an impossible state of invariable relations, the "ideal" goal of re-creating his internal universe as completely independent of empirical proofs.

The process can be seen as moving towards a state of complete independence from the here-and-now of somehow liberating oneself from the insistent physiological necessities of the moment. Scientists and philosophers both seek eternal verities independent of crude biological process. The paradox is that any real attainment of such a state would be incompatible with life for the simple reason that life is a continuously moving, continuously entropy-increasing operation which must continuously be supported by the input of negative entropy ("negentropy" both as energy and information) if the system is to be able to survive. Thus we find the endless paradox of the search for stability and equilibrium even though it is easy to demonstrate that equilibrium and stability are only attainable in inorganic systems, in a limited way at best. Equilibrium is incompatible with life or with learning: forward movement of at least minimal degree is an absolute requirement for any biological system. [1971, pp. 69-70]

Thus the family in crisis, when it comes seeking therapy, is also greatly involved in attaining this "ideal goal," and it would not even come were it not prey to the fear that its equilibrium and stability (defended and maintained against all empirical evidence) were in danger. The difficulties of motivating a family which *does not* feel itself in this danger are much greater.

When we speak of positive connotation, we find ourselves facing a series of contradictions and paradoxes. Earlier we spoke of the necessity of overcoming our linguistic conditioning and its intrinsic moralism. At the same time, to approve and confirm the homeostatic behavior of all the members of the family, we are forced to use language. The very expressions of approval which we use require the use of "moralistic" judgments, the same as if we were using phrases of disapproval.[16]

But it is here that we find ourselves in the paradox of using language to transcend language, and of adopting moralistic behavior in order to transcend moralism, since it is only thus that we can reach the systemic approach in which moralism has no meaning whatsoever.

In other words, by qualifying "symptomatic" behaviors as "positive" or "good" because they are motivated by the homeostatic tendency, *what we are connoting positively is the homeostatic tendency of the system, and not its members.* However, one can approve of certain behaviors of single individuals insofar as these behaviors denote the common intention toward the unity and stability of the group. Through such approval, the therapist not only defines himself as allied with the homeostatic tendency but actually prescribes it.

If we consider the peculiar modes of the family in schizophrenic transaction which have been described in chapter 3, we see that the rule of rules of these families is the prohibition of any definition of the relationship. It is as if the family were metacommunicating to the therapists, "We can stay together only as long as we do not define the relationship. Not defining the relationship is essential to the stability of our system."

Upon reflection, we can see also that the symptom, that is, the psychotic behavior manifested by the identified patient, is, by its very bizarreness and obscurity, an attempt to avoid such a definition. The identified patient, in this sense, *obeys* the rule of rules. But, at the same time, the symptom alludes, in a critical and sarcastic way, as a protest as it were, to a definition of the relationship. In fact, at a higher level of abstraction, a relationship which has been defined as undefinable is, at the same time, defined as untenable.

The identified patient, in this sense, *threatens to violate* the rule of rules. And with this threat, he causes within the group a state of alarm related to the risk of rupture of the status quo.

When the family asks for help, it is seeking the restoration of the equilibrium it enjoyed previous to the outbreak of the symptom. It actually obtains this from traditional psychiatry, since the allusion threatening a new definition of the relationship, that is, a change, is labeled a "sickness" and "treated" as such.

Let us now consider how, and according to which epistemology, we deal with these families when they come to us.

First of all, the therapists make no distinction between the "symptom" of the identified patient and the "symptomatic" behaviors, that is, the peculiar patterns of communication, shared by all members of the family. Do the members of the group in schizophrenic transaction communicate in this way because they don't *want* to communicate otherwise or because they don't *know how* to? To this question we can answer that making a choice would be the same as falling into the illusion of alternatives and would be exactly like trying to decide if the identified patient *can't* or *won't* behave differently. At this point, the therapists "know" one thing only: all the members of the family oppose themselves to any change which presents a danger to their homeostatic ideal, and it is therefore necessary that the therapists ally themselves to this ideal (naturally, for the moment only).

Here we find the therapists doing exactly the opposite of the family. They deliberately ignore the allusive and threatening aspect of the symptom as a protest and invocation to change. Instead they underline and confirm only its homeostatic aspect. Similarly they confirm the behaviors of the other members of the family as striving for the same goal: the stability and cohesion of the group.

In addition to these fundamental functions, positive connotation has two other important interdependent therapeutic functions: (1) to clearly define the relationship among the family members and between the therapists and family without the danger of receiving a disqualification; and (2) to be a context marker, since it defines the context as therapeutic.

In regard to the first point, the family in schizophrenic transaction uses analogic language in contrast to digital language. The transactional patterns of this type of family are characterized by the effort not to define the relationship. Each member refuses to define himself as the one who defines the relationship (and therefore imposes upon the others rules of behavior), just as he refuses the others the right to define the relationship (and therefore to impose rules upon him).

As Haley has shown, and as our own experience has constantly confirmed, the members of the family in schizophrenic transaction disqualify with high frequency all the components of the message: author, receiver, content, and even the context in which it takes place.

In addition to this phenomenon, Haley (1959) has shown two others which are closely related: (a) none of the members of the group is inclined to declare or to truly recognize any leadership within the group; and (b) none of the members is willing to really accept the blame, that is, the responsibility for what goes wrong. We can thus see how the positive connotation transmits, on various levels, a series of messages:

1. The therapists clearly define the relationship between the various members of the family as complementary to the system, that is, to its homeostatic tendency. Finding themselves all in an identical complementary position in respect to the system annuls the hidden symmetric tension present in the various members of the family.

2. The therapists clearly define the relationship between family and therapists as complementary, as they (the therapists) declare their own leadership. This is done not through a direct and explicit communication, but implicitly

through a global metacommunication which has the character of being a confirmation.

In doing so, they communicate that they have no doubts about their own hierarchical superiority. In fact, the authority which approves and motivates this approval, communicates that it has no doubts about itself. [17]
As for the context of such a communication, it can be neither refused nor disqualified by the family members, since it conforms to the dominating tendency of the system: the homeostatic tendency.
Exactly because the positive connotation is an approval and not a reproach, the therapists can avoid being refused by the system. Moreover, the family can for the first time have the experience of receiving an explicit confirmation.
But at the same time the positive connotation implicitly puts the family in a paradox: why does such a good thing as the cohesion of the group require the presence of a "patient"?
Such a definition of a relationship as described in (a) is connected with (b): a clear definition of the relationship, as described above, constitutes a marker of the therapeutic context.
To conclude, we can say that positive connotation permits us to:

1. put all the members of the family on the same level, in that they are complementary in relation to the system, without in any way connoting them moralistically, thus avoiding any drawing of a dividing line between members of the group
2. accede to the system through the confirmation of its homeostatic tendency
3. be received in the system as full-right members, since we are motivated by the same intention
4. confirm the homeostatic tendency in order to paradoxically trigger the capacity for transformation since positive connotation prepares the way for the paradox, Why should the cohesion of the group, which the therapists describe as

being so good and desirable, be gained at the price of needing a "patient"?
5. clearly define the therapist-family relationship
6. mark the context as therapeutic

However, the principle of positive connotation is not entirely free from difficulties when it comes to its practical application. It can happen that while a therapist believes he is giving a positive connotation to all the members of the system, he is making, without realizing it, an arbitrary dichotomization.

This occurred to us in a case dealing with a family of three generations, the identified patient being a six-year-old boy diagnosed as severely autistic. In addition to the child and his parents, the maternal grandparents were requested to take part in the third session.

From the material gathered during this session it appeared to us that there existed a possessive and intense attachment on the part of the grandmother toward her daughter, who, for her part, had contributed to this attachment by finding various ways of being in need of maternal help. At the end of the session, we expressed admiration for the daughter for the sensitivity and kindness she had always shown toward her mother. That this was an error was immediately brought out by the response of the mother, who cried, "So then I'm selfish!" Her indignation revealed the hidden competition between mother and daughter as to which of the two was the more generous. This error gained us the hostility of the grandmother and jeopardized the continuation of therapy.

In other cases, we intended to make positive connotations, which were instead received as being negative. The following case describes this point.

The family consisted of three members: the father, Mario; the mother, Marta; and Lionel, seven years old, who had been sent to us with the diagnosis of child autism. Considering the intense ties maintained by this family with its extended family (as happens in most families with psychotic children), we had requested the presence of the maternal grandparents at the fifth session. In this session we were able to observe a striking redundancy.

The two grandparents had always been, as a couple, ferociously symmetrical. In their feud, the family had divided into two factions: Marta had been taken over by her father, a violent and possessive man, while Nicola, her younger brother, now in his thirties and married, had always been preferred and overprotected by his mother, a meek and seductive woman.

During the preceding sessions, it had already become apparent that Marta, "having already" the love of her father, had yearned intensely for that of her mother, that is, for the pseudo-privileged relationship her brother had always enjoyed. She declared herself jealous of her brother, just as her husband Mario was. Mario, usually impassive and rigid, became animated only when he protested against his selfish and infantile brother-in-law, who, among other things, did not deserve the gratuitous love showered upon him by his mother. The redundancy which struck us in that session was a statement made by the grandmother over and over again, that she felt strongly inclined to love those who were not loved. She had loved and still loved her son Nicola *only because* her husband had never loved him, but had instead given his love to Marta. Now she felt obliged to love Nicola's wife (poor thing, she was an orphan), and she really loved Lionel, her psychotic grandson, most of all, because she had the impression that Marta had never really accepted him. Ever since he had been born (and here her voice trembled with deep-seated emotion) she had noticed how he had been nursed "as if he were a calf."

It became clear during that session what the moral imperative of that "sweet" grandmother had always been, and still was: "to love the unloved" (an obviously symmetrical move). At the end of the session, the therapists took leave of the family without any specific comment and cordially thanked the grandparents for having so kindly collaborated.

In the next session, only Lionel and his parents were invited. Taking into consideration the material gathered from the previous sessions, we began by praising Lionel for his great sensitivity. He had thought that his grandmother, generous as she was, needed to love only those who weren't loved. Since Uncle Nicola had gotten married six years ago and was therefore loved by his wife and no longer needed his mother's love, Granny was left with no one unloved to love. Lionel had understood this situation perfectly, and had realized it was necessary to supply his grandmother with someone unloved whom she could love. Thus, ever since he had been small, he had done everything he could to make himself unlovable. This caused his mother to become more and more nervous, getting angry with him, while Granny, on the other hand, could show infinite patience with him. Only she really loved "poor little Lionel."

At this point in the session, Lionel began to make an infernal racket, banging two standing ashtrays one against the other.

The reaction of Marta was sudden and dramatic: she regarded our statement to Lionel as a sudden illumination of the truth. She added even more to the story by saying that she had actually felt happy when her mother criticized her for rejecting Lionel. "It's true, it's true!" she cried, "I was happy when my mother said I was treating him like a calf. But what can I do now? [wringing her hands] I've sacrificed my son to my mother! What can I do to pay for such a tremendous fault? I want to save my son ... my poor baby!"

We immediately feared we had made a mistake. In fact, not only had Marta disqualified our definition of Lionel's sacrifice as voluntary by redefining him as *her* sacrificial victim, but she also felt that *she* had been defined by the therapists as the "guilty one" who had sacrificed her child to her mother. In this perspective, Lionel returned once again to his position of victim, and his father, as usual, seemed to find it convenient to remain silent, a spectator to something that really didn't concern him.

At this point, after the suspension of the session and the discussion of the team, the therapists decided to involve the father and to put him back in his position as an active member of the system. Upon rejoining the family, we observed benignly how Mario had, in contrast to Marta, presented absolutely no reaction to our comments.

Therapist: "Our provisional hypothesis is that you also must have some very profound motives for accepting this spontaneous sacrifice of Lionel."

Marta (shouting): "His mother! His mother! Lello [Lionel] is even worse when she's around! She has to convince herself that Mario is unhappy with me! That as a mother I'm a failure! My mother keeps telling me that I'm not patient enough with Lello, but she [the mother-in-law] tells me I'm not strict enough! That's why I get so nervous and yell at Lello! And my husband just sits there. He never defends me . . . look at him!"

Therapist: "Let's all think about this until the next session. In the meantime, let's make it clear that Lionello isn't anyone's victim. [turning to the child] Isn't that right, Lello? *You* thought of becoming crazy so you could help everyone. No one asked you to do so. [turning to the parents] Do you see? He doesn't say anything, he's not crying. He's decided to continue to do just like he's done until now, because he's convinced he's doing the right thing."

As we have already said, our first impression, when faced by the reaction of Marta, was that we had made a mistake. She, while agreeing with our comment, communicated that she felt she had been defined as guilty: she was a bad mother who had sacrificed her son to the needs of her unresolved ties to her own mother. The absence of any reaction on the part of the father strengthened our suspicion that he also had interpreted our intervention in that sense: "Since my wife is the one responsible for Lionel's psychosis, I'm good, innocent, and therefore superior to everyone."

However, in a further discussion we became convinced that our connotation of Lionel's behavior had not been an error, but rather a well-directed move which had uncovered a nodal point. What Marta could not tolerate was the idea that her son was *not* a "sacrificial calf" but rather an active element in the family system and, more than that, in the position of leadership. In disqualifying the active position of Lionel, relegating him again to his role as an object, as a passive victim, Marta was working precisely in favor of the preservation of the status quo of the system. She tried to recuperate her lost position of pseudo-power by defining herself as "guilty," and therefore the *cause* of her son's psychosis.

Her reaction was convenient to Mario, whose presumed superiority in the system consisted in the opposite, that is, in his appearing as the good and tolerant one. To keep their covert competition intact and to perpetuate the family game, it was necessary to put the child back into his role as an object.

For the moment we could do only one thing: put Mario in the same position as Marta by saying that he too was motivated by profound needs to accept the spontaneous sacrifice of Lionel. At the same time, we put Lionel in a position of superiority as a spontaneous interpreter of the presumed needs of the family. Thus we were able to prepare the way for the paradoxical prescription of the psychotic leadership of Lionel.

chapter 8

THE PRESCRIPTION IN THE FIRST SESSION

We have found it useful, and very often necessary, especially in families with psychotic children, to give a prescription by the end of the first session. In some cases, we make an apparently innocuous prescription with various goals:

1. to mark the context as therapeutic
2. to provoke within the family a feedback which indicates compliance and motivation for treatment
3. to limit the field of observation
4. to give structure to the following session

As for the first point, that is, the necessity of defining the context as therapeutic, this is a fundamental point, because this type of family is noted for its ability in disqualifying the context as therapeutic. This occurs both in the talkative and "social" family, which behaves in session as if it were attending a party, as well as in the reticent and withdrawn family.

As for the "social" family, we dealt with one, of "high society," particularly gifted in its fantasy and ability to present at every session a new and imaginative disqualification of the therapy. The beginning of the first session, characterized by a series of giggles and laughter, spirited jokes and word games in response to the attempts of approach made by the therapists, could easily have been entitled "A Typical Afternoon at the Club."

At the beginning of the second session, their mood somewhat dampened by an intervention made by the therapists at the end of the preceeding session, the family succeeded in disqualifying the context by posing a series of questions concerning the ideal weight and diet of the identified patient, a slightly obese adolescent girl. We can call this second shift in context "A Chat with Marguerite's Dietitians."

The beginning of the third session was even more fanciful. For ten minutes the family discussed in full, with particular attention to detail, the advisability of attending or not attending the impending funeral of a relative in Liguria.

This we refer to as "A Conference on the Funeral Habits and Customs of Liguria."

As we have stated, the reticent and withdrawn family is no less capable of disqualifying the context of the therapy. Their behavior in the first session is common enough to be described thus: the family sits stiffly in a closely drawn-together group. They fix their eyes upon the therapists with an interrogative expression. Their general attitude is of expectancy and wondering: "Well, here we are, now what do we do?" Looking at them, an outsider would never dream that it is the *family* that has requested this meeting and not the therapists. Their silence and nonverbal attitude is quite clear: "We have courteously come at your kind invitation and here we are to find out what *you* want from us."

Experience has taught us that any interpretation we might make of this attitude of the family only results in a reaction of amazement, negation, and disqualification. Moreover, in attempting to metacommunicate on this behavior, a critical and moralistic connotation would be inevitable. On the contrary, a simple and well thought out prescription, inspired by the redundancies observed during the session, permits us both to avoid any critical or moralistic connotation and to redefine the relationship as therapeutic.

Furthermore, as we have stated in points three and four,

such a prescription serves to delimit the field of observation and to give a format to the following session.

In some talkative families, the second session runs the risk of being an exact repetition of the first, *as if* the family had already said everything of importance and could therefore only repeat itself. In receiving a prescription, the members of the family are constrained in the following session to refer in some way to the prescription.

We can give as an example the following case of a family consisting of three members: the two parents and a ten-year-old daughter presenting a psychotic behavior which had begun in her fourth year. The child, although she had been regularly attending a special school for the past three years, had not yet been accepted in the first year of regular elementary school. During the first session, the therapists observed a repetitive phenomenon: if they asked the child a question, her mother immediately responded for her. Without any comment by the therapists on this behavior, the parents spontaneously explained that their daughter couldn't answer because she was unable to construct sentences and was able to utter only isolated words. At the end of the session, the therapists gave to each of the parents a notebook with this prescription: during the week to come the parents were to write down, with great detail and care, each in his own notebook, all the utterances made by the child. They were to be careful to omit nothing, for a single omission could jeoparadize the therapy.

This prescription was meant to achieve various goals:

1. to ascertain the willingness of the parents to follow a prescription
2. to provide the little girl a new experience: that of being listened to, and of eventually being permitted to finish a sentence (since her parents, intent on recording every word she said, could no longer interrupt her)
3. to provide the therapists important data
4. to base the following session on the reading of the notebooks, thus eliminating meaningless and repetitive chatter

As a side-note to our main topic, we would like to note the incredible follow-up of this session. In our second session with this family, we discovered in the notebook of the mother sentences which were complete, albeit elementary. But in the notebook of the father we discovered a sentence which was striking when one considered the "dumb" behavior shown by the child. This sentence had been uttered while father and daughter were driving alone in the family car: "Daddy, tell me, do tractors have gears too?" What was even more striking than the content of this sentence was the attitude of the father as he read it. Shaking his head repeatedly, he slapped shut the notebook and looked at us in a bewildered manner, sighing, "Just look what this little girl has to say," as if the recorded sentence were unequivocal proof of her insanity.

At this point we must, however, make clear that even an apparently innocuous prescription could lead to errors, if the therapists failed to take into account and correctly estimate certain behaviors indicative of a particular family organization.

We can see a clear example of this in the case of another family which presented as the identified patient a six-year-old autistic boy, as well as an apparently healthy sixteen-year-old daughter. At the end of the first session, we decided to prescribe the recording in a notebook of all the sentences and phrases uttered by the boy. This prescription was to be made, however, to the mother alone, as her husband was a traveling salesman and was to be away on business for the following weeks. Our intention was to make use of this stratagem as a means of separating the couple. The behavior of the family had influenced us to believe (how naive we were!) that by coming alone to the next session, the wife would give us information she dared not give in the presence of her husband. After deciding for these reasons to make this prescription, the therapists rejoined the family to make their final comment and to give the prescription. Upon entering the room, they found the father, who had left his seat, facing them, standing between them and the family with his arms slightly raised at his sides. In other words, he was in the classic defensive position of one whose exclusive possessions are being threatened. Such a clear body message should have warned us of the error we were about to make, but instead we went ahead to invite the wife to come alone to the next session.

The day of that session, we received a call from the husband, saying that his wife could not come, that she was sick in bed. In vain we tried to recuperate this family, but the error proved irremediable.

In other cases, particularly where the family seems not to be motivated, but rather compelled to come by a referring physician, we use interventions intended to put the family in crisis. These are some of the most difficult therapeutic moves and the most exposed to error because these families are firm in their decision to give us as little information as possible.

Such was the case of the Villa family. During the telephone conversation the referring child psychiatrist gave us minimal information concerning the family. Her diagnosis of the five-and-a-half-year-old identified patient was that of child autism. We failed to make further contact with the referring doctor before the first session, thus condemning ourselves to guesswork concerning the family background, which in this case, as we shall see, would have been particularly useful. We did have our transcription of the first telephone contact with the family, made by the mother several months before, requesting therapy.

In this conversation she stated that she had had difficulty in convincing her husband to come to family therapy. She had succeeded in this only because the child psychiatrist, who had been treating their son, Lillo, with medication, had refused to see them again until they had made an appointment at our center. She explained that Lillo's "illness" had begun two years before, immediately after a severe cold. He had changed completely: he no longer played, either alone or with other children. From that time on, he remained quietly in the house, almost as if he weren't there. At times, he cried for no reason. During meals, he had to be fed, since he sat at the table as if in a trance, not noticing the food in front of him. At other times, for no reason at all, he would have tantrums, flinging objects around. In these cases, his mother fed him something and he quieted down.

In the session Lillo had the appearance of a little old man. His skin a faded yellow color, his stomach protruding, he had a sheeplike expression on his face. For most of the session, he remained immobile in an armchair without speaking or responding to any question.

The therapists gathered the following information from the parents. They had married rather late, having met each other at a Catholic matrimonial agency. Neither had had previous sexual experience. They got along immediately, both "simple" and sharing the same ideas. (Here we point out the term *simple*, as it occurred throughout the session ad nauseam.) Their social and cultural level was quite low, and neither had gone past the fifth year in elementary school.

Communicational disturbances of the two were imposing. Any interaction was rendered nearly impossible by continual contradictions and disqualifications. Nearly all sentences were finished with a cryptic "anyway," leaving the therapist who had asked the question with empty hands.

As for their relations with their respective families, it appeared that they had remained relatively distant from the family of the wife, while, on the other hand, they were intricately involved with the family of the husband.

Mr. Villa had lived with his mother and younger sister, Zita, until he was thirty-seven years old. In the same house, which had three stories, lived Villa's two brothers and their wives and children. Both of the brothers had completed technical schools and were economically comfortable.

Nina, the wife, had been well accepted by her mother and sister-in-law, largely because of her "simplicity." To make room for the newlyweds, the mother's apartment had been divided in two by a large closet placed in the central hallway. Until the mother's death, all had gone well, but immediately afterward, Zita had begun to quarrel with her brothers: she wanted to sell them her inherited part of the house (for an exorbitant price) and get out. Nina, who had always tried to please everyone, had been accused by Zita in one of the family arguments, as being the "cause of everything." Nina experienced a tremendous moral shock, and her husband, indignant, couldn't understand how such an unjust accusation could be made of such a sweet and "simple" woman.

Finally, through the intervention of friends, the brothers agreed to pay Zita, who then married and left the family. During this period (preceding Lillo's illness) Nina, depressed and downcast, continually asked her husband to move, and thus get away from the family feud, but failed to convince him. Even after Zita's departure from the field, the relationship between the remaining members of the family remained cold and strained. "The good times were gone forever, when we got together to watch TV in Mama's kitchen." However, in spite of our questions and the answers we received, we had no inkling as to the reason for this coldness. Why had it persisted? Hadn't Zita been the cause of the trouble? Hadn't they all joined together against her? These questions received only vague answers, in the form of the proverb "When you've been burned once, you keep away from the fire." But it was unclear *who* had been burned or *why*.

Lillo's sudden change occurred shortly after Zita's marriage. Our attempts to understand what had happened just before this change were smothered in a mass of contradictions. In the same way, we were unable to discover what the first signs of psychosis in Lillo had been. It was only during this part of the session that Lillo got up from his chair: twice he went to his mother, touching her lightly on the mouth and covering her ears. He never went near his father, who, sitting on the edge of his chair, was on the far side of the room.

In its discussion, the team agreed upon the total lack of motivation in the family to undertake therapy. It was clear that they had withheld important information from us. It would be, therefore, an error to offer them therapy. We felt it essential to define family therapy as being necessary but at the same time, to refuse it, thus pushing the parents to ask for it on their own initiative. But how could we accomplish this?

When the therapists had hinted at the eventual possibility of a change of house, they had met in the couple a wall of resistence: it was impossible, for economic reasons. It was useless to insist on this point. If they could now make up their minds to move, it was clear that they would already have done so. But if the problems of living close to the extended family were really so great, why didn't they leave? Here the best answer we could find was that both were there to get something out of the extended family.[18]

In this complex tactical struggle, Lillo was obviously fully involved. He had most likely received a verbal injunction to be "good" with his relatives and to play with his cousins, while, at the same time, he had received the nonverbal message to keep away from them. Thus placed in a double bind, Lillo had chosen the psychotic solution: keep away from *everyone*.

After this discussion, we decided upon the following therapeutic intervention: we would give the family a letter addressed to the referring doctor, with whom the family had an appointment in two weeks. the letter was not to be a private communication, as is usually the case, but instead was to be read aloud to the family by one of the therapists before handing it over to the father. The letter follows:

Dear Colleague:

In reference to the case of the Villa family, we are in complete accordance with your idea of giving the approximately ten sessions of family therapy. However, at the present moment, therapy cannot be initiated due to one factor: the extraordinary sensitivity of Lillo. We say he is a child of extraordinary sensitivity because, already at the age of three-and-a-half, he decided to no longer play with children whose parents did not appreciate his mother. Since, from what we have understood in our first session, we cannot see the possibility of Mrs. Villa's recovering for the time being the esteem she had earlier received from her mother-in-law due to her simplicity, we don't believe Lillo will be able to start playing again and behaving as other children do. Furthermore, Lillo is so sensitive that, in order to offend no one, he doesn't even play by himself. Only when Mrs. Villa will have some idea as to how she can regain the appreciation and esteem of her relatives, can we speak of making an appointment for the second session.

The letter, read aloud by one of the therapists, provoked dramatic reactions in Lillo. When the therapist arrived at the phrase "Lillo is so sensitive, that, in order to offend no one . . .," his face began to wrinkle up. The observers behind the mirror watched him intently. His chin began to tremble, he clamped his lips seeking to control himself, but finally broke into tears. Abruptly he jumped from his chair and threw himself upon his mother, kissing and stroking her. She, receiving his caresses passively, turned brusquely upon the therapists: "But it isn't as easy as you think. How can I make them appreciate me?"

We thus received a feedback of confirmation from both mother and son, although that of the mother was surprising, since she behaved *as if* she herself had given the information referred to in the letter. The father remained in his place on the other side of the room, silent and unmoving.

When the therapists stood up to dismiss the family, Lillo threw himself on the floor, screaming and kicking, directing looks of hate toward the therapists. His parents had to carry him from the room.

Shortly after this session, we telephoned the referring psychiatrist. During this conversation, we received the information that the psychotic behavior of Lillo had begun two years before with a period of acute agitation, during which he uttered at a rapid rate the same words over and over again: "To move, to move, to move." During a diagnostic interview, when asked by the psychiatrist to draw a picture, he had made one of a courtyard full of people. One of these, taller than the others, was separated from the group and inside a cage.

The psychiatrist said that for the past two years she had spoken to the parents about moving. She had even demonstrated, in black and white, that they could afford such a move (obviously they had other reasons for not changing houses!). For our part, we explained the purpose of the letter, that it had been intended essentially as a paradoxical therapeutic intervention: to submit the continuation of the therapy to the realization of an impossible goal: that of Mrs. Villa's regaining the esteem of her in-laws. The paradox lay in the fact that, if the mother was to regain this esteem, therapy would become unnecessary and Lillo would be cured. But, since this was impossible, the family would find themselves at a crossroads: the choice of giving up the therapy or of leaving the field, that is, of abandoning the pretense of recapturing the lost appreciation of her in-laws.

After a month we received a telephone call from the mother, who said that the psychiatrist had found Lillo improved, and had insisted that the family make an appointment for the second session. However, at the moment, this was impossible, for the family was going on a vacation to the seaside for fifteen days. She added: "I know this won't settle anything, but it's the first time we're going away since we got married. Anyway, Doctor, I'm convinced it's all my fault." After another month she called again: "We brought Lillo back to the psychiatrist. She said he's getting better, but that we have to see you again. My husband won't agree because of the expense. I don't know what to do."

After this conversation we again discussed the case and our therapeutic intervention. Regarding the diagnosis, we felt we were dealing with a psychotic depression in a child. Regarding our intervention, we decided that it, in its essential points, had been quite accurate and correct, and had brought about certain desired results. At the same time we were able to discover two grave omissions we had made. The first had been our failure to directly involve the father. We could have, for example, referred to him in the letter as the one who suffered the most for his wife's loss of esteem. Our second omission, the more serious, was that we had not completed the paradoxical prescription at the end of the first session with yet another paradox: fixing an appointment for a second session. This would have been incongruous with our previous statement that it was impossible to continue therapy. Substantially, the point was to do therapy with a reluctant family while defining this as impossible.

When, by contrast, a family comes to us in crisis, of its own will, and not because of the insistence of a referring doctor,[19] we find ourselves in a quite different situation. In such cases, it is often possible, already in the first session, to prescribe the symptom to the identified patient, with surprising results, as long as care is taken to positively connote the symptom in the systemic sense, allying oneself with the family's homeostatic tendency.

One example of this can be found in our treatment of the Lauro family. The appointment for the first session was made with relative urgency (four weeks after the first telephone contact) due to the nature of the case itself as well as to the insistent telephone calls made by the father, who appeared desperate and at the end of his wits.

The family had been referred to us by a child psychiatry clinic, where the ten-year-old son had been examined and given a series of psychological examinations. The diagnosis was of acute psychotic syndrome in a subject of high intelligence. The boy had been prescribed and administered heavy medications, but without results. In the first session, the father seemed to be a highly emotional man, a bit flaccid in his appearance. The mother, slim and well-kept, showed, on the contrary, a controlled and aloof attitude. Ernesto, their only son, was tall and overdeveloped for his age, but was striking in his peculiar behavior, which could almost be called farcical. He walked stiffly, slightly bent forward, taking short and hesitant steps like those of a very old man. Seated between the parents at an equal distance from both, he responded to all questions talking "staccato" in a high nasal voice. He used difficult and obsolete words alternated with expressions which sounded as if they came from an early nineteenth century novel. For example, he interrupted his father once with the following phrase: "It is advisable that I now intervene with a clarification so that these gentlemen will not be deceived by appearances."

According to his parents, Ernesto's strange behavior had begun suddenly three months before, after a short visit from an aunt. When she had left, Ernesto had withdrawn within himself, often broke into tears for no reason, and frequently clenched his fists in a threatening way, as if facing some invisible enemy.

While he had always been the best in his class in past years, he was now the poorest student. He wanted to be brought to school by his mother in spite of the jests of his classmates, with whom relations were hostile. He didn't want to go out with his father anymore, because he was afraid someone shooting at his father would miss and hit him instead. In spite of his father's denials and protests, Ernesto insisted that they were always followed by a thin, bearded man. "First I saw him from behind and then we were face to face. Since I'm not subject to hallucinations I recognized him perfectly."

We learned that the couple had lived with the wife's family, which was composed of her father and three older brothers (the mother had died years before). Giulia, Ernesto's mother, had to care for the whole family and was always worn out. When two of the brothers finally married, the Lauro family moved into their own home, and Giulia's father came to live with them. He stayed with them for four years until his death, which occurred when Ernesto was six years old. After this death, the family moved again.

Ernesto, according to his parents, had suffered a great deal over the death of his grandfather, to whom he had been very attached. He had always been "smart" for his age, but happy and sociable. After his grandfather's death, he stayed indoors, no longer playing with his friends. He would spend the afternoons after school in his room doing homework or reading encyclopedias. The parents found no complaint in this behavior, as his school work profited from it.

It was only in September, after the visit of his aunt and four years after the death of his grandfather, that Ernesto changed in a sudden and dramatic way. The parents were unable to explain the reason for this change. They could only say that Giulia had had a particularly enjoyable month with her sister-in-law, whom she usually visited in the country during the summer holidays. This sister-in-law had come to town to undergo a series of medical examinations. "It was a happy period because, having always lived only with men, it didn't seem to be true that I was able to stay with another woman, to talk with her about so many things."

The therapists could discover no more than this. They asked what the parents thought about Ernesto's attitude, that is, his way of looking and behaving like an eighty-year-old man, and of speaking like someone out of a century-old book. The father said nothing and the mother answered by saying that Ernesto had always been a precocious child, with a rich and well-developed vocabulary. She admitted, however, that this phenomenon had recently become far more noticeable. At this point, Ernesto interrupted with one of his typical cryptic comments: "This question doesn't surprise me, it doesn't surprise me at all. This has all been pointed out already. I think it's because I don't like summaries [was he referring to the vague and imprecise way in which his parents always expressed themselves?]. I don't ask questions. I read quite a bit. I look for answers in the text. I prefer to read texts."

At this point the two observing members of the team called out one of the therapists. It was clear by now that Ernesto was miming his grandfather. It would be better not to persist in other questions which the family seemed resolutely to evade.

The therapist rejoined the family, and after a few minutes asked Ernesto to tell them about his grandfather, how he had acted. The boy temporized, saying he couldn't remember. The therapist then asked him to show how his grandfather had talked to his mother. After thinking for a few moments, the boy settled himself solemnly in his chair and said: "Oh come on, Giulia, come on" in a tone of benevolent superiority which he accompanied with a gesture which seemed to say: "Cut out the silliness."

After Ernesto had finished this demonstration, the therapist asked him to show how his father spoke to his mother. Ernesto hesitated a bit, then turned to his father saying: "Daddy, I don't want to offend you, but if it can be advantageous. . . ." His father responded with a sign of assent.

Ernesto began in a whining voice: "Giuuulia, Giuuulia . . . I will think about everything. Please now, go take a little nap."

At this point the therapists withdrew to discuss the case with the rest of the team. The two observers remained at the mirror for a few minutes and saw the father agitatedly scold

Ernesto: "But why did you say that to the doctors?" To which the boy replied, "So that they'll know that you're good, as good as gold."

In the discussion which followed among the therapists, the prevalent hypothesis was that Ernesto, caught in the middle of an unreconcilable couple, had become aware of some danger immediately after the death of his grandfather. By closing himself up in the house to read and study, he was trying in some way to take his grandfather's place. However, with the arrival of his aunt, the danger of a change, perhaps of a threatening coalition between the two women, must have appeared to him to be much greater.

The team agreed that basically Ernesto was more attached to his father and was convinced of his father's inability to assert himself, to take a masculine role, and to counterbalance the increasing maternal power. To strengthen the homeostasis, Ernesto had resuscitated his grandfather, the only one who had been able to control his mother, to keep her in her place. More than this, for the moment, the team was not able to understand. It was decided, therefore, to close the session with a positive connotation of the behavior of Ernesto, without any criticism of his parents but with a cryptic and nonverbal allusion to a certain fear he had for his father, that is, for his father's possible eventual defeat.

This comment was prepared minutely, not only in its verbal but especially in its nonverbal aspects, because the therapists thought it imperative to avoid naming the mother and the father and their presumed difference of position in the family. The suspicions of the team were immediately confirmed when the therapists rejoined the family, by the change of Ernesto's position: he had pushed his chair closer to that of his father and had moved it somewhat forward, almost blocking him from the therapists' view.

First the therapists announced their conclusion that it was necessary to proceed with family therapy, which would be carried out in ten sessions, at monthly intervals.

Ernesto (always in the voice of an old man): "But your response, what is your response?"

Male therapist: "We are closing this first session with a message to you, Ernesto. You're doing a good thing. We understand that you considered your grandfather to be the central pillar of your family [the hand of the therapist moved in a vertical direction as if tracing an imaginary pillar]; he kept it together, maintaining a certain balance [the therapist extended both hands in front of him palms down, both at the same level]. Without your grandfather's presence, you were afraid something would change, so you thought of assuming his role, perhaps because of this fear that the balance in the family would change [the therapist slowly lowered his right hand, which corresponded to the side where the father was seated]. For now you should continue in this role that you've assumed spontaneously. You shouldn't change anything until the next session, which will be January 21, five weeks from now."

After the delivery of this message, the therapists rose to their feet to see the family out. The parents seemed lost and confused. But Ernesto, after a moment of shock, jumped suddenly from his chair, and, abandoning his octagenarian attitude, ran toward the female therapist, who was leaving the room; grasping her arm, he cried: "and school? You know that at school I'm a disaster. Did you know that? I might get left back. Did you know that?

Female therapist (gently): "For the moment you're so involved in this generous task you have chosen to carry out, that it's natural you don't have any energy left for school. How could you?"

Ernesto (shouting, with a desperate expression on his face): "But for how many years do I have to repeat the fifth grade until I can make them get along, for how many years? And will I be able to? Tell me!"

Female therapist: "We'll talk about all this on January 21. The Christmas vacation is coming."

Mother (very disturbed): "But I couldn't tell you what happened in September. I wanted to say . . ."

Male therapist: "We'll talk about all that on January 21."

Father: [disqualified everything by asking for trivial advice].

This first intervention already proved correct in its immediate feedbacks. In the second session we were able to note other changes. Ernesto had given up his old man's behavior, even though he still expressed himself in a literary and dated fashion. For the past two weeks he had been taking advantage of school and he no longer spoke of bearded men who followed him. These changes permitted us to receive more information and therefore to form new interventions, which in their turn produced new changes and new information. And thus we continued for ten sessions, which resulted in meaningful changes in the couple, and naturally in Ernesto. The seventh session of this family will be spoken of later, in chapter 11.

chapter 9

FAMILY RITUALS

Another of the therapeutic tactics orginated by our team, one which has proved particularly effective, is that of prescribing a ritual to the family. We have prescribed rituals which are to be carried out only once, as well as others which are to be repetitive.

Of the several effective family rituals we have prescribed to date we choose to present one particular example, which had as its goal the destruction of a myth whose existence was created by the members of three generations. So that the reader may have an adequate understanding of this ritual, we shall describe fully the story of the family and of the transgenerational evolution of this myth. In the description of the treatment of the family, certain errors made by the therapists shall come to light, errors which, as usual, were far more instructive than the actual successes. For eventually it was the very understanding of these errors and their feedbacks which led us to the successful prescription of the ritual. Finally, the detailed analysis of the substance and goal of the ritual shall illustrate and explain exactly what we mean by the term. For this case history, we shall give the family the fictional name of Casanti.

A RITUAL AGAINST A DEADLY MYTH

Our story of the Casanti family begins during the first years of this century, on a large and isolated farm in a depressed area of central Italy. For many generations, the Casantis had sweated a living out of this land, of which they were not the owners, but tenant farmers. The head of the family was the "Capoccia," an iron-fisted worker who based his uncontested authority upon a long tradition of patriarchal rules, which were in fact modeled after those of the feudal era. His wife could have stepped from the pages of *The Books of the Family* written by Leon Battista Alberti in the late 1400s. A tireless and parsimonious worker, she was convinced that the role of the woman was to serve, give birth, raise children, and never question the superiority and rights of men, having as her only reward her own virtue. She had given her husband five sons. Siro, the youngest, was to become the father of our family.

For these people, when you were born a peasant, you died a peasant. The work was hard, and there was no time for pleasure or holidays. Although the five sons learned to read and write in the village school, they were needed to work in the field. Every helping hand was precious, and no one could be excused; there existed absolutely no alternatives. What else could an ignorant farmer do anyway, but stay with his family and help support it and put away some savings for the common good whenever possible? In unity there was strength, or at least survival. No protests on the part of the sons were tolerated, or even permitted. The only thing was to settle down and join the others.

In the 1930s in the Tuscan Maremma, the patriarchal family was still isolated and considered by its members to present their only assurance of survival and dignity. To leave the family meant emigration and uprooting, without any means or preparation. It meant doing without help and support in case of illness or hard luck. Needless to say, most families, including the Casantis, chose to remain together.

In this culture, a father with sons was fortunate. Not only would he have help in the fields, but he would have daughters-in-law, who, obedient and industrious, would work in the house as well as in the fields. Thus, each of the sons was encouraged to marry early, as soon as he reached the proper age. The bride would come to live with her husband's family, and submit herself to the authority of her father-in-law, her husband, her brothers-in-law, and any sisters-in-law who had preceded her, in that order. The Casantis patterned themselves after this age-old tradition.

The first four brothers had already been married for some time and had settled down to family life when Siro, the youngest, returned from the war. He had been away for several years, from 1940 to 1945, had fought, and had seen many things never dreamt of at the farm. He had also received training as a mechanic and had a truck driver's license. When he was discharged from the army, he returned to the farm, and found himself depressed and estranged. For some time he was unable to get involved in the work, and was treated for mental exhaustion. He gradually readapted himself, and was able to join the others as he had years before.

Soon the "Capoccia" began to nag him. It was time he got married. Two of the daughters-in-law were pregnant, and the family needed a woman who could run the kitchen and care for the livestock. They had already chosen a candidate, the daughter of a neighboring farmer. Siro, however, had other ideas. He remembered Pia, a lovely dressmaker he had met in Florence while serving in the army, and decided to look her up. Pia was not quite as he remembered her. Once lively and gay, she had become wilted and sad. She had been abandoned by her fiancé after years of engagement, and felt her chances for love and romance were over.

Nevertheless, Pia accepted Siro's proposal, going against the advice of her friends and relatives. ("You won't be able to stand that kind of life. You'll see, you'll come back to us soon.") But Pia knew she would never go back. For her, it was almost like going into a nunnery. The Casantis, after much hesitation and doubt about the "city girl," finally accepted her. They understood she was a serious girl and would work hard and never complain.

But times had changed. The family was full of tensions. With the increasing impact of the industrial boom, which had finally succeeded in reaching the most isolated regions of Italy, they began to have contacts with the outside world. They listened to the radio, and going to the market saw all manner of strange things. The daughters-in-law, accustomed as they were to their position in the family as chattels and servants, were amazed when they saw elegant women who smoked and even drove cars! They began to complain of old "Capoccia," who never relaxed his authority, as well as of their mother-in-law, who sided with "her" men. For example, only the men were allowed to go into town on Sundays, while the women were expected to remain home cooking and caring for the livestock. They began to complain about these restrictions, the most courageous actually trying to convince their husbands to leave the farm. But, in the face of this danger, the five sons joined their parents, forming a silent coalition. They, the sons, were the "true" Casantis. It was their responsibility to control the women of the family. There was no place for complaint, expression of dissatisfaction, or jealousy. It had to be clear that there was no inequality in the distribution of jobs and expenses: everything was done with complete equity. And as for the children, it was likewise forbidden to make comparisons, or to express judgments. Rivalry was unthinkable, the children of one were the children of all.

Thus was born the family myth of "one for all and all for one," a myth shared also by anyone who had contact with the family. "No other family in the whole region gets along like the Casantis. Such a big family, and everybody loves each other; no fighting, no bickering. . . ."

Pia, Siro's wife, played a large part in the building of this myth. The last to arrive (and therefore under the authority of all the others), she was considered by her mother-in-law a saint, no small achievement in such a culture. She was the wise one, always the helpful one, the impartial mother of all the children of the clan. In her own children she had been unfortunate, giving birth to two daughters in this family where sons were prized. She treated them with the same care she gave her nephews and nieces, without showing any preference. In fact, in cooking and distributing food, she always served her own children last. Sometimes her daughters found her crying in her room, but when they questioned her, she always answered that she had a headache, or didn't feel well. If her husband, returning from the fields, complained that the hardest work was always left to him, she sought to calm him, telling him that he was mistaken, that the life was equally hard for everyone.

At this point, we can observe how all the characteristics of the family myth, as described by Ferreira (1963b), are now present. In the first generation examined by our inquiry, that is, of the "Capoccia" and his wife, we observe the existence of a belief which is still vital in the context of the reality of a patriarchal farming subculture, homogeneous in its isolation: "The survival, safety and dignity of its members depend on the family. Whoever separates himself from the family, is lost."

In the absence of alternatives, information, and confrontations, there is no conflict. But when the second generation, that of Siro and his brothers, reaches adulthood, disruptive tensions begin to appear. The fascist era with its glorification of the graingrowers is over, and democracy, with its political rallies, arrives in even the most isolated villages. The work of the tenant farmer is defined as humiliating and exploited. Industrial culture imposes itself through movies, the radio, markets, and the inevitable contact with people who can "make money fast."

But the Casanti brothers, still led by the old Capoccia, are suspicious. These are all signs of a world gone mad. Their strength is always the old one—to work hard and to be united. To stay together, they must create a myth, a collective product whose very existence and persistence should be able to reinforce the homeostasis of the group against any disruptive influences.

Like all myths, as Ferreira points out, this one "imposes upon its adherents certain limitations which end in gross distortions of reality. In consequence, the myth modifies the perceptive context of the family behavior, in that it supplies ready-made explanations of the rules that govern the relationship within the family. Furthermore, the myth in its content represents a detachment of the group from reality, a detachment which we can at this point call "pathological." But at the same time, this myth constitutes, with its very existence, a fragment of life, a part of reality which confronts, and thus forms, the children born within it.

The myth of the Casantis, by now consolidated and extended to the third generation, survived the death of the Capoccia and his wife, as well as the eventual abandoment of the farm. Toward the end of the 1960s, due to the crisis in the position of the tenant farmer, the five brothers decided to leave the land and transfer themselves to town. They were ex-farmers, uncouth and uneducated. How could they possibly separate, divide their hard-earned savings into minuscule portions? Far better to stay together and found a business which could profit from their common abilities.

They organized a construction company, which immediately profited by the building boom. For the first time in their lives, they had plenty of money: they could begin to enjoy the pleasures of a consumer society. They could live in apartments in town. Here again the myth presided; they all moved into the same apartment building. Although they had separate apartments, their doors were always open to the others of the clan, even to unannounced visits.

With the growth of the third generation, the situation became even more complicated. The myth had to become more rigid, since expectations had changed, and disruptive tensions had become more intense. The petit bourgeois, which made up the society in which the Casantis now found themselves, was fraught with confrontation and competition. Children were compared according to their success in school, their physical attributes, their friendships and popularity. Jealousy and envy occurred with each confrontation. News and gossip flew from door to door; windows became listening posts.

The Casanti myth had rigidified to the extreme. Even the Casanti cousins were true brothers, they shared their joys and sorrows. Together they suffered the failure of another; together they rejoiced in the luck of another. The iron rule, never mentioned, forbade them not only any comment but also any gesture that could be said to be motivated by jealousy, envy, or competition.

When Siro moved with the clan to the city, his daughters were fifteen and eight years old. Zita, the eldest, had always been a tomboy. Dark, stocky, and loving the country and physical activities, she suffered from her new conditions of life. She studied, not because of enthusiasm or amibition but because it came easily to her. She lived estranged from her surroundings, disappointed in city life, and dreamt only of returning to the country some day. During her sixteenth year, for some months, she manifested an anorectic syndrome, from which she recovered spontaneously.

Nora, the second daughter of Siro, was still a little girl. Completely different from her sister, she passed her days with Luciana, her cousin, who was also her classmate. Nora was closer to Luciana than to her own sister. Luciana may have been skinny and homely, but she was lively and ambitious, and always the first of her class. Nora, on the other hand, showed no interest in schoolwork, and felt no envy at the success of her cousin.

At thirteen Nora underwent a dramatic metamorphosis. Always a pretty child, she became an extraordinarily beautiful girl. Completely different from the rest of the family, she seemed a Madonna of the Tuscan Renaissance. Her father, Siro, became fiercely proud of her. He kept in his wallet a photo of his daughter and showed it to everyone whenever he could. Nora, on the other hand, seemed hardly pleased by this turn of affairs; in fact, she reacted nervously to any compliments on her beauty. Together with Luciana and the other cousins and friends, she was urged to go on outings or to go to dances every Sunday. She returned nearly every time depressed, without being able to explain why.

In school, things started going badly. Even when she studied, she was unable to answer the questions put to her. Shortly after her fourteenth birthday, she suddenly stopped eating. In only a few months, she was reduced to a skeleton and had to leave school. Three periods in the hospital, as well as an attempt at individual psychotherapy, had no effect. Due to the advice of a local psychiatrist, the family made contact with our Center.

In January 1971 the first session took place. As was our practice at that time, we made a contract with the family for a maximum total of twenty sessions. The sessions were to be held every three weeks or more, according to our judgment. The family accepted. The trip, due to the distance they had to travel, involved a great sacrifice. They would arrive after an entire night spent on a train, only to repeat the trip as soon as the session was over.

At the beginning of the therapy, Siro, the father, was fifty years old, Pia, the mother, forty-three. Zita, who was nearly twenty-two was enrolled in the University of Siena, but was not taking any courses at the time. Nora, fifteen, was a frightening skeleton, five feet nine inches tall, and weighing seventy pounds. Her behavior was psychotic. Completely removed from what was going on in the session, she limited herself to moaning, repeating a stereotyped phrase every once in a while, "You should make me gain weight without making me eat." We learned that for months she had left her bed only in order to indulge herself in bulimic orgies, which were inevitably followed by bouts of vomiting which reduced her to prostration.

The first part of the therapy, which took place in nine sessions, from January to June, was characterized by these outstanding factors:

1. the insistence of the therapists, after the second session, in inquiring into the relationship between the members of the nuclear family and the entire clan;

2. the ironic attitude of the therapists in regard to the myth, and their attempt to attack it openly through verbal clarifications, as well as through naive prescriptions intended to force the family to open rebellion against the myth;

3. the nonsystemic conviction, both linear and moralistic, that the true slave to the myth was the father, and not, as it actually was, all the members of the family;

4. the attempt, obviously unsuccessful, during the sixth and seventh sessions, to call only the three women of the family, hoping that in the absence of the father, they would open up;

5. the failure to point out, as could have been done after the review of the tapes of each session, a peculiar redundancy: every time a member of the family, apparently allied to the therapists, criticized the clan, there was always another member ready to minimize or disqualify what was being said, or to divert the discussion to some marginal topic;

6. the progressive abandonment of her symptom by Nora from the fourth session to the sixth, when she presented herself in flowering physical condition;

7. the suspicion of the therapists that Nora also, with her improvement, was defending the system (which in effect had not changed), and the incapacity of the therapeutic team, on their part seduced by this improvement, to come out of the impasse.

At the end of the ninth session, the therapeutic team decided to halt the treatment, declaring that the goal desired by the family had been reached. Although there still remained eleven sessions, Nora was in excellent condition, and had started work as an apprentice in a beauty shop. In reality, we wanted to sound out the family. If the improvement of Nora was false, the therapists would still have eleven sessions to work with. A telephone appointment to report Nora's progress and to discuss the general state of affairs was agreed upon for the fifth of September.

The call was made punctually by the father. Nora was well, but had given up her work, and tended to stay by herself at home, separated even from her parents and sister. Siro's tone was cryptic, uncertain. He asked the therapists if another session was indicated. The therapists left the decision up to the family, who, although they agreed to discuss the issue and call back, failed to do so.

The team, however, did not expect the dramatic events which followed. Toward the end of October, the father once again called the Center. Nora had attempted suicide and was in the critical ward of the local hospital. They had found her on the bathroom floor in a state of coma induced by alcohol and barbiturates. Its being Sunday, she had returned in a depressed state from a local dance where she had met her cousin Luciana.

Upon finding herself alone in the apartment, she had profited from the absence of her family by taking this tragic step.

In the session which followed Nora's release from the hospital, the family, by now at the end of its tether, let some important information escape. The father confessed that the clan had shown itself hostile in September to the idea of the family's return to therapy. They felt it was completely useless for Siro to lose valuable time and to spend so much money now that Nora was cured.

Zita, the sister, made an important revelation. Perhaps, in Nora's drama, Luciana had played an important part. During the summer, Nora had confided in her sister that for years she had felt persecuted by her cousin. She had said she was afraid to stay with Luciana, and was nervous and anxious in her presence, even though she didn't know why. But Zita went on to disqualify what Nora had told her, as well as her own revelation of it, by adding: "Maybe this is all only an impression of Nora."

While Nora remained silent, the parents took up the defense of Luciana. She was a true sister to Nora, full of love and concern. In fact they had been struck painfully by Nora's lack of receptiveness, by her reluctance to accept the insistent and affectionate invitations made by Luciana.

But this time the therapists refused to take the carrot offered them. Even if certain members of the family seemed willing to make revelations, the therapists this time had no intention of falling into the same trap. The session was halted while the entire therapeutic team met to discuss the new turn the situation was taking. The errors made in the first sessions had become clear. Going against such an iron-clad myth had served only to strenghten it. Insisting upon change had only succeeded in arousing fears of the breakdown of the system, and had constrained Nora to abandon her symptom in order to reinforce the status quo. In reality, nothing had changed.

Since Nora herself was a participant in the myth, she had ended up by doubting the reality of her own perceptions. How could she dare to think that Aunt Emma and Luciana didn't love her? Perhaps she perceived Luciana as being hypocritical, envious, and evil only because she, Nora, was all of these things.

The team decided, therefore, to refrain from any verbal comment. It was urgent that we invent and prescribe a ritual, making use of the dramatic situation so that it would be followed. At the same time, it was necessary to prescribe the "pathology," that is, the fidelity to the myth, while reassuring the family and putting it at the same time in a paradoxical situation.

The two therapists, returning to the family, declared themselves extremely preoccupied by the dramatic situation, but above all, by the emerging hostility toward the clan, which endangered the accordance and well-being of the whole group. It was of vital importance that nothing escape and of equal importance that the family commit itself to follow the prescription the therapists were about to give. The family, duly impressed, agreed to do so. The prescription was as follows.

In the two weeks that were to precede the next session, every other night, after dinner, the family was to lock and bolt the front door. The four members of the family were to sit around the dining room table, which would be cleared of all objects except an alarm clock, which would be placed in its center. Each member of the family, starting with the eldest, would have fifteen minutes to talk, expressing his own feelings, impressions, and observations regarding the behavior of the other members of the clan. Whoever had nothing to say would have to remain silent for his assigned fifteen minutes, while the rest of the family would also remain silent. If, instead, he were to speak, everyone would have to listen, refraining from making any comment, gesture, or interruption of any kind. It was absolutely forbidden to continue these discussions outside of the fixed hour: everything was limited to these evening meetings, which were ritually structured. As for relations with members of the clan, a doubling of courtesy and helpfulness was prescribed.

The ritual, as can be seen, had several goals:

1. to define the nuclear family as a unit distinct from the clan, substituting for the prohibition, the obligation of speaking clearly about the tabu subjects, while at the same time imposing the keeping of secrecy

2. to give back to Nora her position as a full-right member of the nuclear family

3. to encourage the newborn intragenerational alliance between the two sisters

4. to establish, without explicitly saying it, the right of each member to express his own perception without being contradicted or disqualified

5. to expose any eventual reticent member to the anxiety of silence

6. to prevent, through the prohibition of discussion outside of the evening meetings, the persistence of secret coalitions [20]

The prescribing of reverence toward the clan qualified the therapists as being allied to the family's homeostatic tendencies and placed the family in a paradoxical situation. In fact, they found themselves confronting an unexpected about-face on the part of the therapists in the very moment when they were ready to accept that the clan was endangering their existence and the survival of Nora.

The family carried out the ritual and two weeks later presented itself greatly changed. Nora, hardly recognizable, told how much she now understood of the maneuvers of Luciana, who had always made her feel guilty for any success. Luciana was able to do this without commenting openly, by withdrawing into silence, by showing herself as being depressed, by demonstrating a certain coolness toward Nora. It was as if Nora's successes were an offense to Luciana.

Pia, for her part, had "discovered" how much Aunt Emma (Luciana's mother) was consumed by envy to the point of making life impossible for everyone. Siro intervened, saying that Luciana's and Emma's behavior was due to ignorance not to "badness." Nora replied that she too felt somewhat "bad" to have said what she had of Luciana.

But the rule was broken, and it was finally possible to metacommunicate about it: "Whoever speaks *badly* of his relatives, is *bad*." The therapy had finally touched the system's nerve center and changes followed in great leaps. Once the field was cleared of the myth, it became possible to work with the family's internal problems.

HOW TO DEFINE A FAMILY RITUAL

From the formal point of view, the term *family ritual* refers to an action or series of actions, usually accompanied by verbal formulas or expressions, which are to be carried out by all members of the family. The ritual is prescribed in every detail: the place in which it must be carried out, the time, the eventual number of repetitions, by whom the verbal expressions are to be uttered, in what order, etc.

A fundamental aspect of the family ritual concerned our specific preoccupation with the approach to the family in schizophrenic transaction: how to change the rules of the game, and therefore the family epistemology, without resorting to explanations, criticism, or any other verbal intervention. As Shands says, the basic idea can never be stressed often enough "that there is a necessarily complete difference between the objective world and the world of symbolic process, between the doing and the naming, between the level of action and the level of description" (1971, p. 30). And again:

> The relation between behavior and description is in a certain way similar to that which occurs between the circular motion of an automobile's wheel and the linear projection that can be designed on a map to show the path it followed. Behavior is always a controlled process of a circular motion (with feedbacks) of messages between central and peripheral mechanisms, in which the continual input of information from the periphery is at least as

important as the flow in the other parts of the circle.
[Shands 1971, p. 34]

This agrees with what Piaget showed in his studies of the
epigenetic evolution of the human being:

> The capacity to carry out concrete operations precedes the
> capacity to carry out formal operations; the capacity to
> "centralize" the perceptive processes precedes the ability
> to "decentralize" them, that is to carry out abstract
> operations. The phase of concrete operations is therefore
> the necessary premise to the phase of formal operations.
> In other words, to arrive at a digital code, it is indispensa-
> ble to have a previous analogic adaptation. However, once
> the individual has arrived at the level of formal operations,
> the two processes, analogic and digital, blend, and cannot
> be distinguished except through a linguistic artifice.
> [quoted in Shands 1971, p. 34]

The family ritual, especially in that it presents itself on the
level of action, is closer to the analogic code than to the digital.
This preponderant analogic component is, by its nature, more
apt than words to unite the participants in a powerful
collective experience, to introduce some basic idea to be shared
by everyone. One thinks of the widespread use of rituals in the
mass education and conditioning of the New China. Contrary
to the slogans, catchwords, and phrases to which an individual
can render himself impenetrable, rituals are much more
successful in introducing, for example, the basic idea of union,
cooperation, and complementarity to the common good. Every
ritual becomes valid (in the passage from sign to signal, and
from signal to norm) because of its normative function, which
is inherent in every collective action where the behavior of all
the participants is directed toward the same goal.
    We can therefore conclude that our prescription of a ritual is
meant not only to avoid the verbal comment on the norms that
at that moment perpetuate the family play, but to introduce

into the system a ritualized prescription of a play whose new norms silently take the place of old ones.

The invention of a ritual always requires a great effort from the therapists, first an effort of observation, and then a creative effort, since it is unthinkable that a ritual proven effective in one family can be in another. It must be specific for one given family, in the same way as certain rules (and therefore a certain play) are specific for each family in a given here and now of its curriculum vitae, which includes, of course, the therapeutic situation. Finally, we want to point out that the prescription of family rituals has proven itself extremely useful also in the treatment of families manifesting types of interaction other than the schizophrenic.

chapter 10

FROM SIBLING RIVALRY TO SIBLING RESCUE

In this chapter, we describe a type of therapeutic intervention which has shown itself particularly effective in families
which have more than one child, and which present one of
the children as the identified patient.

With this intervention, we arbitrarily shift the label of "sick"
from the identified patient to one or more of his siblings who
is or are considered by the family to be "normal." We point out
that the identified patient is the only member of the family to
have understood his sibling's true position and condition,
which is far more alarming than his own, and that it has been
his conviction that he alone can help them. In doing this, we
avoid any criticism or blame of the parents. We say that we are
impressed by the sensitivity and comprehension demonstrated
by the identified patient and that, from the material we have
gathered and the observations we have made during the
session, we find ourselves in complete accord with him and are
quite concerned about the supposedly "sane" sibling. From
data acquired, we can demonstrate that the "normal" sibling,
behind his facade of security, happy-go-lucky superficiality,
obedient behavior, or nonconformity, as the case may be, is
in reality, pseudoautonomous: he is attempting unconsciously
by these means to keep his position of being preferred by one
or the other of the parents, who on their part have no inkling

as to these intentions, much less as to how to be able to thwart them.

We continue, saying that this unconscious attempt to obtain and maintain such a position of preference is very harmful to its author: it prevents him from growing and becoming autonomous. Only the identified patient, thanks to his extraordinary sensitivity, has, for quite a while, understood the danger in which his sibling finds himself. The patient has developed his "illness," that is, his behavior, which in various ways limits his own existence and growth, thereby attracting the attention and preoccupation of his parents to himself. He implicitly urges his sibling to take advantage of this situation in order to free himself and become truly independent.

We positively exclude the possibility that the identified patient is doing anything for himself: he is not at all interested in getting the favor and approval of anyone. His purpose is truly altruistic.

As we have already said, this intervention can be used only when a family has more than one child; we first successfully applied it to families with anorectic patients, and later to many other types of families presenting a patient identified as neurotic or psychopathic. Once we began our research on families in schizophrenic transaction, the shifting of the "sick" label to the supposedly "healthy" proved itself valid more than ever as an intermediary tactic, intended to provoke confusion in the family ranks.

This confusion is frequently expressed in immediate and dramatic feedbacks in the defense of the status quo, and has proved catastrophic if we permit ourselves to be intimidated or swept away by the fear of having made a mistake. Such feedbacks occur in many forms: anguished telephone calls about the real or presumed worsening of the identified patient (as if to say: "Enough of this fooling around, *he's* the sick one!"); requests for earlier sessions or for individual appointments; and self-accusation on the part of the parents. Feedbacks of this nature had, during our first experiences in using this intervention, the pragmatic effect of throwing us into doubt, and in consequence, anxiety and incoherence, to the point of inducing us to abandon the intervention and thus nullifying any effect it had thus far accomplished. There are frequent attempts during the following session to disqualify everything previously said by various methods, from the detailed description of the "patient's" symptoms (as if this were again the first session) to the classical disqualification of total amnesia (*Therapist*: What effect did our comments of the last session have on you? *Patient*: My Goodness! What comments? We said so many different things).

The negative feedbacks of the "amnesia" type provoked within us a sense of confusion ("But we said it clearly enough, why didn't they understand?"), or else an intense irritation or depression, powerful enough to betray us into making punitive responses.

It took us time to understand that the feedbacks coming from these families are negative precisely because this type of intervention strikes a powerful blow against the status quo, which is founded on the officially declared belief that in these families, made up of normal members, there is, inexplicably, a disturbed member. Beneath this, there is likewise the belief, not officially declared, that the identified patient is "crazy," at least in part, because he is envious and jealous of his "healthy" siblings. All this is mixed with a secret sense of guilt that the identified patient isn't entirely to blame, since there are, or have been, in the family's relationships, certain preferences whose very admission is prohibited.

Here it is necessary to make a clarification. Sibling rivalry is a common and normal phenomenon, just as the different relations between each parent and each child are common and normal. This does not produce any significant dysfunction as long as such differences are clearly defined.

In these families, the hidden symmetry between the parents is ramified, in an equally hidden manner, in the younger generation. In fact, the difference in the relationship between each parent and each child is instrumentalized for the purpose of the game and, therefore, disqualified and denied any time there appears a danger of its being brought into the open. The result is, as an effect of this game, that there is inevitably one who feels appreciated and one who feels unloved. In this way, the hidden battle between the pseudo-privileged and the pseudo-neglected guarantees the perpetuation of the game; on the one hand by the pseudo-privileged, who attempts to maintain his position (of pseudo-power), and on the other by the pseudo-neglected, who attempts to attain a position he has never had. All of these maneuvers and attitudes are hidden in an intrigue of secret and denied coalitions which cannot easily be broken up.

We can give an example of such a situation in the case of a family presenting a psychotic adolescent with two much older sisters. We needed several sessions in order to understand that the identified patient had secretly allied herself with her father and the second-born sister in order to punish her mother for the preference she had always shown toward the eldest daughter, Bianca. Using covert psychotic behavior, the identified patient had succeeded in forcing Bianca to leave home.

We were able to overturn the family epistemology by designating Bianca as "sick" (depressed and inactive, she had been living for months in the country in the home of two old aunts, her only solace being daily and lengthy telephone conversations with her mother), while we admired the sensitivity and sacrifice of the identified patient who, by her behavior, tried, if with little success at the moment, to force Bianca, already twenty-eight, to fulfill herself outside the family.

Later in the therapy, we began to demonstrate that not even Bianca could be said to be disturbed. She was only a sensitive and generous girl who had taken too seriously certain heart-to-heart talks her mother had had with her concerning her father. As a result of these talks, she had believed her mother to be very unhappy and in need of her companionship. However, we said, this need was not at all apparent to us therapists. The mother, as we saw her, could only want, more than anything, that Bianca disattach herself and become an independent woman. (These words were greeted by a cry of confirmation from the mother.

This therapeutic tactic has proved itself most useful in producing changes within the family, only when we are able to resist the immediate negative feedbacks previously described. The figures of the parents are temporarily pushed into the background while the therapists bring the younger generation to the fore of the stage. It is with the game that occurs between the members of the younger generation that the therapists begin their tactical change of the punctuation.

The pseudo-privileged suddenly becomes the disadvantaged, since in allying himself to one of the parents he prevents his own growth. The therapists are careful in basing their intervention upon concrete information brought by the family, and upon observable behaviors which occur during the session, and *not* upon their own hyptheses or opinions.

Once the family shows itself willing to accept this inversion of the punctuation (whose reality is as undecideable as the previous one), the therapists change their punctuation again and bring the parents back to the forestage. We say that the child who wanted to make a coalition with, for example, the mother, was not doing it for herself but for her mother (as when Bianca refused to become independent), basing this action upon the erroneous conviction that her mother needs this sacrifice. In our opinion, we continue, the mother has no such need, and as in the case of Bianca's mother, she can only confirm enthusiastically what we have said.

We have spoken of this tactic as being an important intermediate maneuver intended to undermine the status quo of the family system. In fact, seeing that the family's dysfunction is perpetuated by the belief that his family is basically healthy but in some mysterious way contains a "crazy" child, by declaring that the crazy one is not that child but rather his sibling or siblings, we reduce the dilemma to two alternatives: either everyone in the family is crazy or there isn't anyone crazy at all.

The dilemma, if everything works well, resolves itself in the second alternative: there isn't anyone crazy at all. *There was only a crazy game* which had absorbed all the interests and energies of the family. From session to session the game becomes less and

less powerful, finally dissolving, without the therapists ever
having spoken of it, and with it disappear all the peculiarities in
behavior which had made it up and guaranteed its perpetuation.

chapter 11

THE THERAPISTS TAKE UPON THEMSELVES
THE DILEMMA OF THE RELATIONSHIP
BETWEEN PARENTS AND CHILD

In the previous chapter we mentioned the particular difficulty we face when treating a family in which the identified patient is an only child. This difficulty lies in the fact that we face a twofold danger: that of being stimulated (often with the cooperation of the child) into criticizing the parents, as well as that of being enticed into the coaltions and factional battles which are part of the hidden symmetry of the couple.

Only after undergoing a series of frustrating and fruitless experiences were we able to find an effective solution. This solution consists of referring exclusively to ourselves the intragenerational problems in a manner similar to that of transference interpretation made in psychoanalytic treatment. The difference is that this is done in the presence of the parents, who cannot help but take into account the implicit allusion to their intrafamilial problems.

Referring to ourselves the intragenerational problems is tactically advantageous, since the parents find themselves in a position where they can neither deny nor disqualify. Who is talking about *them*?

We can give an example in the seventh session of the therapy of the Lauro family, already mentioned in chapter 8. The reader will remember that the ten-year-old son, Ernesto, had experienced a psychotic crisis which caused the family to come to us. After the first session, which took place shortly before the Christmas holidays, Ernesto (as a result of the therapeutic intervention) had abandoned his florid psychotic behavior and taken up his school work with excellent results. At the same time, however, he persisted in exhibiting behaviors which caused his parents anguish. The behavior which disturbed them most was his obstinate refusal to play with his classmates after school, to make friends, or to go to play in the nearby sports field.

For the first five sessions (one each month), Ernesto had participated in the therapeutic work with great interest and enthusiasm, always showing a great deal of intelligence in his reactions and responses. However, in the sixth session he showed himself to be in a "bad mood" and did not cooperate in the work. While he usually seated himself exactly between his parents, during this session he sat by himself, on one side of the room. He hardly spoke, and when he did it was only to make meaningless or trivial comments, with an air of boredom toward both his parents and the therapists. When his parents spoke of their anxiety concerning his physical indolence, that is, his refusal to go out of doors and to play with other children, he responded with sighs and other expressions of impatience.

At the end of the session and during the team's discussion we attempted to bring into focus this new phenomenon: the radical change in Ernesto's behavior and in his attitude toward the therapy. Reaching no satisfactory hypothesis, we decided to close the session with a lapidary prescription, the immediate and definite suspension of the medication which had originally been prescribed by the referring neurologist. We were sure that such a prescription given without any explanation, would provoke illuminating feedbacks from the group.

In the seventh session (which took place at the end of June) Ernesto presented himself more bored and uninterested than ever. Once again he seated himself at one side of the room. His parents began immediately to complain of his behavior. As for his final report at school, they could make no complaints for he had been promoted with the highest grades in the class. His behavior at home, however, had become worse than ever, and worried them greatly. Shortly after the last session, he had begun once again to clench his fists, as he had done at the height of his crisis, and to cry for no reason.

Frightened, his parents had begun to give him his medication again, although they felt quite guilty about not having consulted us in this decision. They had felt it absolutely necessary, at least until the end of the school term. Even with his medication, according to the parents, Ernesto had continued to behave disastrously at home. When school finished, he no longer wanted to wash or dress himself, but remained in his pajamas all day long, lounging in bed or in an armchair reading comics. When he wasn't reading, his parents often found him in his room, sitting hunched over, his head in his hands. When his mother worriedly asked him what was wrong, he always responded that he was "thinking." Every day was marked by a series of battles to get him to wash, to go out, to go to the sports fields. In this last month they had succeeded only once.

Worried about Ernesto's bouts of "thinking," his parents agreed to take turns keeping him busy, in distracting him. When his mother, exhausted, went to take a nap, it was his father's turn to take a break from his nearby office and return home to play chess or cards until it was time to wake the mother, and so on, all day long.

After they had described all this to the therapists, the mother turned in anguish to Ernesto: "You have to tell Mommy the truth, Ernesto. Are you doing all this just to contradict us, or do you have some other reason?"

Ernesto, who until this moment had remained silent, answered that it wasn't his fault if he wasn't able to go out. His tone was infantile, querulous, whining. His father closed this part of the discussion with a question directed to the therapists: "What we want to know from you today is this: are we behaving in the right way with Ernesto, or are we doing wrong? Should we be doing something different?"

In the discussion following the session, the team was unanimous in the decision to avoid the trap set by the group, that is, the intention of all the parties, especially through the question of the father, to get us involved in their intergenerational feud. Obviously, it was impossible to avoid answering such a question, but it was imperative to avoid entering into its content. Only in this way could we save ourselves from the disqualifications which were more than predictable.

At this point we found it indicated to base our intervention on the rapport between Ernesto and the therapists. The team prepared the intervention in every possible detail, and tried to predict any possible immediate feedbacks, so as to avoid falling into unexpected traps. We expected, for instance, that Ernesto would do his best to get the therapists to criticize his parents. Most likely he was already angry because they had not yet done it.

Here follows the transcription of the conclusion of the session:

Male therapist: "A little while ago, you, Mr. Lauro, asked us a very important question: if you're right or wrong in behaving as you do with Ernesto. Our answer is that it doesn't matter one way or the other..."

Father (interrupting): So you mean that I'm wrong?"

Male therapist: "Not at all. I said it doesn't matter what you do, one way or the other, because Ernesto's problem is with us, not with you. [pause] And why? Because Ernesto hasn't really understood what we therapists want from him or, better yet, Ernesto thinks that, as therapists, even if we don't say it, we are really thinking: 'When will Ernesto grow up, when will he become a man?' And here is his problem with us: if he grows up, in reality, he hasn't grown up at all, because, in growing up, he's only obeying our order, like a child. According to us, this is the problem Ernesto thinks about all day, the problem he has with us. And in effect, he's right. We are prisoners of our role as psychotherapists and therefore we can only want Ernesto to grow up. It's a real problem that blocks all of us. We have seen that Ernesto, in order to become a man, has chosen in the past his own model, that of his grandfather. Maybe now, in order to grow, he should think of another way of his own..."

Ernesto (interrupting and suddenly becoming a lively and intelligent participant in the discussion): "You're saying that if

I grow like you expect me to, I don't grow because I don't really make [shouting] my *declaration of independence!*"

Male therapist: "Exactly."

Ernesto: "But it's the same for them [indicating his parents with his thumb]. They're involved in this story too....these guys!"

Male therapist (avoiding the danger of slipping into a criticism of the parents): "It's a complicated matter, Ernesto. Let's look at the story of your going back on medication. At the end of the last session, we ordered the suspension of medication, right? It was an implicit message that we considered you ready to grow, actually it was almost an order. And you began to cry, to feel sick, and your parents gave it back to you. This shows that your problem was, and is, with us. In making them give you back the medicine, you communicated that you want to decide *yourself, when* to grow, and *how* to grow. I wouldn't say this is a spirit of contradiction, rather, as you say, it's a declaration of independence in regard to us."

Ernesto (aggressively): "But then what should I do about the medication?"

Female therapist: "Decide yourself whether nor not you should take it."

Ernesto (petulantly): "Then I decide right now that I'm not going to take it anymore!"

Male therapist (rising to end the discussion): "The next session will be after the summer holidays, the third of September. Ernesto will have time to think about his problem with us."

During this exchange, the mother had never said a word, but from the tense expression on her face, she seemed quite struck by what had been said. Ernesto, once again lively and social, cordially shook hands with the therapists. The father, instead, remained behind in the room to stutter, "But...but then...? Can you give me any hope?" To which the therapist responded with a simple gesture in the direction of Ernesto, who had already left the room, behind his mother.

At this point, we can imagine that the reader is asking himself the why of this firm decision not to enter into direct discussion of the relationship between the parents and the child. A fundamental reason has already been given in chapter 7, which deals with positive connotation. Responding to the request of the father and entering into its content could have had only two alternative results: (1) arbitrarily punctuating the behavior of the parents as the cause of the behavior of the son, and therefore criticizing them; or (2) arbitrarily punctuating the behavior of the son as willfully provocative, in this way connoting the son in a negative manner.

In either of these alternatives, it is clear that the therapists would have been disqualified either immediately or in the following session by the son, who could easily disqualify the illusion of alternatives, declaring (as he had done already with his mother) that it wasn't his fault if he behaved as he did, that he couldn't do anything else, or by the parents, who would have returned irritated and depressed to the following session, declaring that their attempts to behave in a different way had achieved no results.

This reason, though fundamental, is not the only one. In the first years of our research, we made the repeated and obstinate error of believing that an adolescent couldn't get "better" unless one was able to change the intrafamilial relationships, especially that between the parents. In order to accomplish this, our only course was to enter into the problem in a direct and verbal manner, interpreting everything that occurred during the session, in the intergenerational relationship as well as that between the couple, with the intention of changing whatever was "wrong."

Besides the fact that in doing so we only succeeded in receiving negations and disqualifications, and, at best, a superficial progress, our more serious error lay in the implicit message we were directing to the adolescent: the condition sine qua non for his own growth was the parents' change. We had not yet understood that the symmetric pretense of "reforming" the parents makes up the core of adolescent disturbances, psychotic disturbances included. As a matter of fact, there does not exist a disturbed adolescent who is not convinced that he is doing poorly because his parents are in some way wrong. The parents have the same belief, with this variant: each is firmly convinced that the true fault is in the other partner.

It is important to note that in *rigidly* dysfunctional systems such as those in psychotic transaction, the children (not only the identified patient) seem to willingly assume the role of "reformers": by indicating an oppressed parent, by tying down a potentially fugitive parent, or by trying to take the place of an unsatisfactory one. We observed an extreme case of this last in an adolescent girl who went so far as to adopt the role of an "ancestral father," that is, by becoming violent, vulgar, and uncouth in order to take the place of a father who appeared weak and ineffectual.

A role thus willingly assumed is also assigned by the system, although always in a hidden manner, through secret coalitions and factions which are immediately denied or dissolved according to the requirements of the game.

The task of the therapists is to behave in a manner as to destroy this false belief that the parents must be changed before the child can grow, to overturn the mistaken family epistemology through an inverse message. This message must succeed in stating that it is not the task of the children to improve the relationship between their parents or to substitute for them in their functions, that an adolescent can successfully grow up and become mature regardless of the type of relationship between his parents.

The essential point is that the adolescent convince himself that his parents' relationship is none of his business. However, such a healthy conviction can hardly develop in an adolescent if in family sessions he must witness the therapists bringing pressure upon his parents, urging them to change their behavior. He has already done this himself for many years. Little wonder that in such a situation, certain identified patients deserted the therapy after a few sessions. They could as well take some time off, seeing that someone else was doing their job for them!

The height of our naivete was that we believed that besides relieving the adolescent of his unpleasant role, we were also offering the whole family an example of what good parents should be. In reality, however, we were only behaving as disturbed adolescents, eager to give their parents failing grades.[22]

chapter 12

THE THERAPISTS ACCEPT WITHOUT OBJECTION
A QUESTIONABLE IMPROVEMENT

This therapeutic maneuver, exemplified in chapter 9 ("A Ritual Against a Deadly Myth"), consists of our accepting, without objection, an improvement such as the disappearance of a symptom which is, at the same time, not justified by a related change in the transactional patterns of the family system. The suspicion arises that this improvement is no more than a move in which all the members of the family are accomplices, although the identified patient may serve as their mouthpiece. Their common intent is to evade a burning topic and defend the status quo. The main characteristic of such an improvement is that it is sudden and inexplicable, accompanied by a carefree attitude and a certain optimism—*tout va très bien, Madame de la Marquise*—which is in no way substantiated by convincing data. With this attitude, the family implicitly conveys to the therapists its collective intention to catch the first departing train, that is, of getting out of the therapy as fast as possible.

In this case, where it is clear that the family is trying to take control of the therapeutic situation, the therapists cannot lose the initiative. A possibility would be to interpret the meaning of this family behavior as a "flight into health." In our experience, however, this would be an error because it implies a critical attitude completely contrary to the principle of positive connotation, and therefore provokes denials and disqualifications or, worse yet, a symmetrical battle. Furthermore, as we have seen in the case of the Casanti family, this urge to flee often follows some therapeutic error or some intervention which, although correct in itself, is premature and intolerable to the group.

Instead, we meet this threat of the family's withdrawal by accepting the improvement without objection, taking to ourselves the initiative of ending the therapy, remaining cryptic and elusive in our attitude.

Since the family has not yet gotten to the point of explicitly requesting termination, but is still involved in the preliminary maneuvers leading up to it, we decide ourselves, from our position of authority, to suspend therapy. The first purpose of such a step is that of always keeping a firm hold on the initiative and the control of the situation, preventing and annulling the move of the "adversary." Our second purpose is directly linked to the terms of our contract with the family: the agreement upon a precise number of sessions. In the face of an inexplicable disappearance of the symptom of the identified patient, accompanied by the attitude of collective resistance described above, we prefer to end the therapy immediately in order to test the authenticity of this "recovery," while having at the same time a number of sessions in "reserve" in case the "recovery" does not bear up under the test of time.

We said that our attitude in this situation is cryptic and elusive. This is because we do not permit ourselves to express in any way our opinion concerning the presumed improvement; nor do we confirm it. We limit ourselves to a simple comment, in which we "recognize" the family's satisfaction with the results of the therapy, and that we have decided the therapy should end with the present session. We stress, however, our obligation according to our contract, to concede to the family upon request the sessions not yet used up, *if* the family should have any need of them.

This therapeutic intervention provokes within the family typical feedbacks, which although they may vary in intensity, bring the family move into the open. One typical response is the question "But what do *you* think?", a question intended to lead us into a discussion of our doubts and objections, which would then be readily disqualified. Instead, the therapists insist that they are basing their decision upon the apparent satisfaction expressed by the family. Thus the family finds itself in the position of being credited for the initiation of a decision which in reality has been taken by the therapists.

Another reaction to this intervention is a sepulchral silence followed by protests and expressions of doubt, uncertainty, and pessimism, and finally an insistence upon making an appointment for another session or obtaining from the therapist at least the solemn promise that an eventual request for an appointment will not necessitate a long period of waiting.

Regardless of the family's reaction, the therapists remain firm in their decision to discontinue the therapy, leaving the family the initiative to request the remaining sessions but with a minimum of time established before such a continuation can be considered. Through such a paradoxical tactic, we are able to annul the threatened sabotage by putting the family in the condition of having to request, sooner or later, the continuation of the therapy.

This type of tactic can also be used with other types of families, for example, with young couples with a patient in early childhood or preadolescence. At times, in such cases, if one is able to obtain the quick disappearance of the symptom of the child, the parents show immediate signs of wanting to escape from the therapy. In this case also, we prefer to avoid any insistence, criticisms, or interpretations. Experience has shown us that such shared resistance is insurmountable. In these cases, we respect the parents' resistance, taking to ourselves the initiative of interrupting the treatment, always leaving open the possibility of an eventual return to therapy. This attitude on the part of the therapists reinforces the parents' sense of freedom in regard to the therapy. Needless to say, the results obtained with the child give them a certain trust in the therapists. In fact, various of these couples have presented themselves after a period of time, to discuss with the therapists their own problems (without the excuse of a child's symptom).

In other cases, while terminating the therapy, we make a telephone appointment or a session within a few months, with the purpose of receiving news and having a follow-up. With this move, we are able to keep the family "in therapy" while we implicitly communicate our continuous interest and availability.

chapter 13

HOW TO COPE WITH THE ABSENT MEMBER
MANEUVER

Among the various maneuvers used by the family to safeguard the status quo, that of the absent member is well known and already described by various researchers. Sonne, Speck, and Jungreis (1965), the first to dedicate a specific study to this subject, concluded that this maneuver, although carried out by only one member of the family, and apparently on his own initiative, "is in reality a total family maneuver, in which the rest of the family collaborates."[23] However, as for the means of preventing such a maneuver, or of foiling it once it takes place, these authors have no suggestions, stating that further research is necessary.

Our opinion, based upon direct experience, is in agreement with the conclusion of these authors: the absence of one or more members of the family is due to a resistance shared by the entire family, with the difference, however, that we believe it absolutely necessary to include in the dynamic analysis the behavior of the therapists and any error they may have made (since they are an integral part of the ongoing system).

We found these errors were most often due to the moralism insidiously present in the therapist's role and goal, that is, in his tendency to offer better models of behavior, and therefore to appear on the side of change rather than of homeostasis.

In the first years of our research, the repetition of such errors resulted frequently in a negative feedback signaled by the withdrawal of one of the members of the family. We then found ourselves in the embarrassing position of having to recuperate him in order to go on with the therapy.

Naturally, unaware of the errors that were the cause of such a feedback, we could only make more mistakes. Thus, time after time, we found ourselves trying to recapture control of the situation with authoritarian attitudes and behavior: "Our patient is the family, we won't accept you for the session unless you all come."[24]

Or else, we would assume an attitude of false nonchalance or, more frequently, would examine and interpret in great detail the meaning and motives for the absenteeism, without, naturally, arriving at any solution. The absent member remained absent, or showed up from time to time, according to his whim, in the guise of a long-awaited guest, to be greeted by questions and interpretations of his motives for having stayed away as well as for having returned ! Needless to say, all such interpretations could be—and were—easily disqualified.

As we were able to understand and eliminate our more obvious mistakes, this phenomenon of absenteeism became more and more rare. All the same, it still occurred occasionally, either as a result of some less obvious error, which we immediately tried to clarify during the team discussion, or as the result of a particularly pertinent therapeutic maneuver which proved premature for the family's acceptance.

As we have said, family research, especially that of the family in schizophrenic transaction, can proceed only through trial and error. The important thing is *to carefully consider every feedback as an output of our own behavior*, and to keep it as a guide to our future behavior with the family.

As for our more recent behavior during sessions, we have given up any authoritarian attitude and any attempt to make inquiries. When a member is absent, we accept the family as well as the motives, usually absurd, trivial, and generic, which they put forward to explain the absence. (He can't ask permission to leave work; he doesn't get along with his boss. He doesn't want to miss school; he has a test today. He doesn't want to come; he says he doesn't have faith in the therapy, that he doesn't see any results. Etc., etc.) Regardless of our apparent acceptance, we see this absence as a maneuver against the therapists and the therapy, and we are especially attentive to what happens in that session, *tying it up to the material of the previous session.* The problem of the member's absence becomes for us the focal point of the session.

The tactic we have developed to recuperate the absent member of the family is intimately linked to the ritual we follow during the session. This ritual, described in chapter 2, divides the session into five parts: the presession, the session, the team discussion of the session, the conclusion of the session with a comment or prescription, and the final team discussion in which the session is recorded. The comment or prescription, given during the conclusion of the session, is usually immediate, and made to the entire group. In the case, however, of a family in which one of the members absents himself, we prefer to withhold the comment or prescription. To proceed as normal would mean giving in to the family maneuver and thereby losing the therapeutic context and role. According to *Pragmatics of Human Communication* (Watzlawick, Beavin, and Jackson 1967), one communicates not only through what he *says,* but through what he *does.* Any comment made to the subgroup would therefore imply acceptance of its self-definition, a definition which does not agree with that made under the original therapeutic contract.

With the purpose of overcoming the obstacle presented by absenteeism, we have in such cases added to the session a sixth part: the conclusion of the session shall take place in the family's home, when *all* the members are present. The concluding comment is, therefore, discussed and agreed upon during the discussion, and written out, signed, and placed in a sealed envelope. Upon rejoining the family, the therapists announce, without any explanation as to why, that the session will be completed that evening, at home, when all the members of the family are present. To one of the members, previously chosen, is consigned the envelope, which he is to open and read aloud in the presence of the entire family. If this is not possible the same evening, the opening of the envelope is to be postponed until such time as all the family can meet together. Through this move, we are able to foil the family's maneuver, while at the same time the absent member is made present.

It is pleonastic to point out the difficulty of writing the comment: every word must be carefully weighed, especially since its purpose is *to involve the absent member to the point of constraining him to return to the sessions.* At times, due to the difficulty of finding exactly the right words, in order to avoid keeping the family from waiting for hours, we decide to send the conclusion by registered mail, giving the family specific instructions as to its eventual reading (by whom, when, etc.).

A team discussion which is drawn out and exhausting, but without a satisfactory result, is a clear sign of our confusion (a state easily provoked by the family in schizophrenic transaction). In this case we find it beneficial to wait for a few days and to let our ideas settle before meeting again to compose the written message.

This tactic has an intense effect of dramatization. When the therapists rejoin the family to consign a written comment rather than making the usual verbal comment, they are often greeted by a dramatic silence, a clear expression of surprise for the failure of the family's maneuver. The effect of dramatization is further heightened by the imposed period of waiting and expectation during the interval between the closing of the session and the reading of the letter at home, and, if we have done a good job in writing the letter, its content will achieve maximum impact.

We used this tactic in the case of a father who did not show up for the fifth session as a result of "a progressive and overwhelming feeling of mistrust in regard to the family therapy." By "coincidence," the mistrust revealed itself just when visible improvement could be seen in the identified patient.

This was a family of four members with two children: Duccio, a boy of six years and Ugo, the identified patient, thirteen years old. At the age of four, Ugo had been diagnosed at a university clinic as a psychotic pseudo-obligofrenic, and had been treated at a neurological clinic as well as by an individual psychotherapist, with no discernable results. It had been this psychotherapist who, exasperated by the impossibility of establishing rapport, had suggested family therapy at our center.

In the first session, the boy presented himself as a moron. Obese, feminine, slouched down in his seat, he kept his mouth open constantly, and wore the expression of a simpleton. To any question directed to him, he either made no response or answered with meaningless, nonpertinent, or cryptic statements. In school he was tolerated, regardless of his poor work and strange behavior, due to the social prestige of his father as well as the influence of his family doctor. Without any friends or interest in sports, he was, however, a champion in chess. When not at school, he spent his time following his mother about. He suffered from frequent and abundant encopresis, soiling his bed and clothing.

The family regarded this as a shameful secret and tried to keep it from even their maid. As a result, the mother found herself spending a good deal of the day hiding and secretly washing Ugo's linens and clothing.

In the fourth session we could detect in Ugo a discernable improvement. He appeared to be lively and interested in the session, with a certain acumen and sense of humor, all of which provoked a visible sense of surprise in the father. We were *not* informed, as we discovered later, that Ugo's encopresis had stopped some weeks before.

The fifth session was scheduled for one month later, but the family did not show up. One of the therapists telephoned to ask for news of the family. The mother answered, greatly embarrassed as well as surprised that her husband had not gotten in contact with us from his office to cancel the session. He had refused to come, claiming a growing and overwhelming mistrust in the therapy as well as an unwillingness to undergo such a long trip (they came over four hundred kilometers from southeastern Italy) and the financial losses incurred by this distraction from his professional activities. She said that Ugo had received his father's news desperately and had closed himself in his room to cry. When the therapist asked her what *she* thought of the therapy, she answered that she was mixed up as well as preoccupied by the reaction of her husband, whom she had no desire to contradict. She agreed, however, to consider the matter and to discuss it further with him at the right moment.

A fortnight later, she telephoned the Institute. Her husband continued to refuse to return to therapy, but had no objection to the others coming. She, personally, wanted to come with Ugo to discuss certain problems concerning his school. The principal had said he was willing to promote Ugo, even though his grades were failing, provided this was in agreement with the opinion of the therapists(!!!). She added (to our complete surprise) that Ugo, "who had become really clean" (something they had omitted to mention in the last session), had slipped back and become even worse in his encopretic behavior.

After a team discussion, the therapists called back to give the requested appointment to the mother and Ugo. This seemed the only way we could eventually get the whole family back in therapy.

In the fifth session, Ugo presented himself as he had in the first: dull, distant, and bored. The mother began the conversation with a vague, almost indifferent afternoon-tea style, touching on the particulars of their trip and Ugo's problems at school. She spoke of his encopresis only when the therapists asked about it (they didn't mention the fact that they hadn't been informed of the previous disappearance of this sympton when it had occurred), and ended by saying that she had *had* it, to the point of having forced her husband, with the threat of leaving him for once and for all, to get a small apartment in Florence, her hometown, where she still had friends, and where she could go every once in a while. The session, after the team discussion, was concluded by the therapists by an appointment for the next session and the announcement that a registered letter would be sent home, addressed to the father, to be read by him in a plenary meeting of the family.

We were not very optimistic that the father would carry out our instructions, but we did not consider this important. It was enough that he read the letter, even by himself, and return to the family sessions. We trusted the curiosity of the mother and Ugo for the message. The written comment was as follows:

> We have been struck by the dedication of Ugo, who, without having been asked by anyone, has made it his duty to reassure his father. In fact, Ugo has the idea that his father is afraid that his wife will leave him. As a result, he has assumed the responsibility of "pinning down" his mother by playing the fool and by dirtying his pants. To this conviction he has generously sacrificed his adolescence, friends, sports, and school. In fact, we can predict that, seeing the apartment in Florence as a threat, he will redouble his efforts to be the fool and to be even more dirty, thus pinning down his mother even more.

At the following session, the entire family appeared, with the father seated slightly to the side, with a very embarrassed expression. Perhaps he was afraid that the therapists would scold him, asking him the reasons for his absence or for his return. Of course, they did no such thing.

They had already prepared a new surprise, a session dedicated to Duccio, the supposedly "sane" child.

chapter 14

GETTING AROUND THE DISCONFIRMATION

As we have said, disconfirmation of oneself and of the other in the relationship ("I do not exist, therefore you do not exist," and vice versa) is the fundamental maneuver used by the family (or any other natural group) in schizophrenic transaction for avoiding a definition of the relationship.

Dealing with the maneuver is the most important and difficult task facing the therapists. In fact, before trying any intervention, the therapists should become expert in the "schizophrenic game," and be fully able to appropriately and systemically use the therapeutic paradox. This implies a series of premises, which, at first consideration, may scandalize the reader, but which have proved indispensable in carrying out interventions with any probability of success.

Above all, the therapists must have learned to play in as detached a manner as possible, as they would in a chess tournament in which little or nothing is known about their adversaries. The only important thing is to understand *how* they play, in order to adjust oneself consequently.

To carry out this therapeutic tactic, we must be freed from any of the motivations which might have influenced us in the choice of our profession: be it the romantic desire to give and help, or the less romantic need for "power." We know that either of these motivations is no more than the expression of our own deeply rooted symmetric premise, a premise which renders us sensitive, vulnerable, and ready to *believe* the manipulations of the family in schizophrenic transaction, so well trained in enticing others into its web. If we are able, instead, to convince ourselves that everything demonstrated to us by the family is a move, whether seductive or disqualifying, we will succeed not only in being reasonably inaccessible to the corresponding reactions of pleasure or anger, but also in enjoying ourselves and in considering our "adversaries" with an authentic admiration, respect, and liking. How many times we found ourselves literally routed by, for example, the family of a modest postal clerk, his wife an illiterate, his son the designated patient who had seemed completely deteriorated, only able to marvel, laughing over and over again ("Fantastic, they're really fantastic"), realizing once again that great gamblers do not need academic education.

However, much time passed before we could laugh in amusement without feeling ridiculous or guilty. Feelings of anxious zeal, of rage, of boredom and futility, of hostile disinterest ("if they want to stay like this, that's their problem) are a sure sign of the symmetrical involvement of the therapists.

Having succeeded in overcoming this barrier (often created by our feelings of "pity" or "compassion" for our patients— "poor things, they are suffering and we do nothing for them") we found ourselves no longer getting completely ensnared by the schizophrenic game, and the checkmate we experienced allowed us to scale down our own hubris. The full understanding of our limitations and of the abilities of our adversaries certainly made us reevaluate our own pretention. There was little to pretend in the face of such overwhelming forces!

As for our weapons, we felt somewhat like David, who in his battle with Goliath had only his sling and a stone and the benefit of a long and diligent experience in target practice, although we had neither the biblical inspiration of David nor the assurance of divine aid in our undertaking, which was far more modest and hardly rated exaltation. For us it was enough to acquire the spirit of the game, dedicating ourselves to becoming experts, never underestimating our adversaries, being ready to lose without getting angry either with ourselves or with our teammates, and, above all, enjoying ourselves.

This is the same as coming to the paradoxical conclusion that the only way *to love one's patients* is *by not loving them*, or, better, by loving them in a metaphysical way. We speak of all this because we feel it our duty to help others wishing to follow the same path—a useless undertaking, since most people have to learn from their own experiences and mistakes before arriving at any given conviction.

The following case was one in which we used the therapeutic intervention of "attacking" the disconfirmation.

The family was made up of a young couple, Luigi and Jolanda, who had been married years, and their two sons, six-year-old Bruno, diagnosed by his referring specialists as autistic, and three-year-old Chicco, who appeared "normal."

The session which we are referring to was the tenth, and therefore the last of the series we had assigned the family.

Ever since the first session, we had been induced to concentrate on the intricate relations maintained with the extended family of the couple (in search of clarification, we once invited the maternal grandparents to a session), without being able to see, for quite some time, how these "intricate extended relationships" had the fundamental goal of confusing and obscuring the central problem of the nuclear family: the relationship between husband and wife.

In the ninth session, the therapists decided to stop this maneuver through a prescription. At the end of the session (following, as always, a team discussion), the therapists consigned a letter to the family, which was to be read during the period before the next session, which was to take place in a month. The reading of the text was to be ritualized in the following way: it was to be read every Thursday by the mother and every Sunday by the father, in the evening, just before dinner, and no comment was to be made after its reading. The text was worded so that it could be read meaningfully by both the mother and the father, without any need for variation. The intention of the letter was to once and for all define the nuclear family *as separate and distinct from the extended family,* clearing the field of grandparents, brothers, sisters, and in-laws, thus forcing the couple to face the threat of a reciprocal definition of the relationship. From this move, which we considered to be strong, we expected an equally strong and therefore revealing feedback. The text of the letter was as follows:

> Now Bruno, I understand why you are acting crazy: to help Daddy. You've decided that he is weak and that by himself he isn't strong enough to control Mommy. So you do everything you can to keep Mommy busy and pinned down, and even Chicco helps you with his tantrums. Since you're taking care of the job of controlling Mommy, Daddy has more time for his work, and can take it easy.

The various reactions of the family came as expected in the next session. Luigi, the father, impassive as usual, but with a livid face, declared immediately that the prescription had been followed but with no noticeable effect on Bruno. Jolanda, trembling and in visible anxiety, said she had suffered terribly. The children had been more unbearable than ever, and even Luigi, for the first time, had been anxious.

When asked by the male therapist about her reason for this crisis, Jolanda referred to the reading of the letter. The text had provoked an incredible flashback, *a complete return to the past!* She had thought about the parents of her parents, about her family's history, about her father who had always shouted at her and never let her do anything, about her mother who cared only for her younger brother, Carlo, and made her, still a little girl, be his baby-sitter and his companion. She had hated to do this, and today, Bruno was only another Carlo for her. *Her family had pinned her down,* always, she had never been free! At the same time she knew that this session (the tenth) was to be the last, and she had felt more anxious as it came nearer. She had the terror of being abandoned. To feel closer to the therapists, she had obtained a book written by Doctor Selvini (the female therapist) and had read over and over again the part that contained the diary of a patient. She had felt that *she* was that patient, even to the point that, in certain details. . . Here she broke down crying.

Male therapist: "Thus, Jolanda, the letter made you think of us. But what do you feel about us?"[25]

Jolanda (suddenly calm, with an inviting smile): "I have to be sincere with you, Doctor. For me, you're still a shadow. But Doctor Selvini is inside my heart! When she smiles at me, it's everything for me. The smile she gives me when she says hello, at the end of the session . . . that helps me."

Male therapist: "And you, Luigi, what do you feel about us?"

Luigi: ". . . I think of you as two nice people . . . um . . . I really couldn't say . . . [decided] I can't say that I have hostile feelings toward you."

Male therapist: "But what reactions did you have when you read the letter? Jolanda told us, and you? What did you think?"

Luigi: "Nothing special.... You said that I am weak.... It's true, but what can I do about it? [he shrugs his shoulders]"

Male therapist: "Jolanda told us that you were anxious, it was the first time that..."

Luigi (in a disqualifying tone): "Anxious...well, I suppose you could say that I was influenced by seeing Jolanda so upset...and then the possibility of finishing the therapy in this situation...it was a possibility just a little..."

Jolanda: "You were anxious, more than me!"

Male therapist: "And you, Jolanda, what did you feel for Luigi? What did you think after reading the letter?"

Jolanda: (as if surprised): "What did I think? . . . I think he should be . . . now I'll tell you something that will make you . . . [laughing childishly, covering her mouth] . . . I think he should be what my mother was never able to be for me . . . and, if by chance he could—which is impossible—I would devour him . . . destroy him."

During this sequence we notice how, for the first time, Luigi had taken upon himself the responsibility of disciplining Bruno. Several times he had gotten up to make the child sit down. As for Bruno, we were able to note that he hadn't gotten worse at all, but that in fact there was an improvement in his attitude and behavior. In the past few sessions he had already abandoned the echolalia and inarticulate cries he had presented in the first sessions. In this session he presented himself as hyperative, obeying for only a few moments, playing with the ashtrays, leaning from the window, while Chicco imitated him as far as possible. The parents had told us after the second session that Bruno had changed his choice of victims: he no longer tormented women, but men.

Comment. The behavior of both members of the couple appeared to the therapists to be no more than an all-embracing maneuver intended to fend off the danger of a definition of their relationship. In fact, in the letter consigned to the family in the ninth session, the therapists had for the first time isolated the nuclear family and alluded to the existing interactional play. The feedback was a maneuver characterized by various moves.

The first, carried out by the father at the opening of the session, was a disqualification which can be translated in the following way: "We faithfully followed your prescription, which had absolutely no effect on the only patient you should be treating, that is, Bruno. Therefore, your prescription has failed."

The following move, carried out by each member of the couple, was a typical schizophrenic maneuver: to extract from the text a single word, and manipulate it in such a way as to disqualify the definition of the relationship with the respective partner, and with Bruno.

Jolanda had isolated from the text the phrase *pinned down*, ignoring the reference to Luigi and Bruno. A mysterious flashback had even carried her back two generations! Through this tactic, she had succeeded in excluding both her son and her husband from the interaction: how could they pin her down when she had already been pinned down by others? Furthermore, Luigi isn't really Luigi, but he is her mother, or rather, he should be *what her mother had never been for her*. If he were ever able to fulfill this role (recognized by Jolanda as something impossible) she would devour him. As for Bruno, Jolanda really doesn't exist, for when she is with Bruno, she is really with Carlo, her younger brother. In the present, Jolanda has one great love, the female therapist Doctor Selvini, who, unfortunately, is no more than someone who smiles at Jolanda at the end of every session, while Doctor Boscolo (the male therapist) is no more than a shadow (who knows that he won't become flesh and blood if the therapy were to continue? In the meantime, let him remain on the sidelines training himself, preparing himself for the eventual combat. He still has some hope of proving himself).

With this final and splendid move, Jolanda succeeded in communicating to the entire group (on various levels and with various goals, one being, obviously, the splitting of the therapists) her desire to continue the game. The therapists, on their part, were able to experience firsthand the seductiveness of the schizophrenic game, whose fascination can be so alluring.

As for Luigi, he had chosen to take out of context the word *weak*, making it lose its meaning. He completely ignored the letter's reference to his desire to "pin down" Jolanda, as well as the allusion to his hidden coalition with Bruno. As for his feelings about the therapists, he could only say that he had no hostile feelings. Thus, he was able to disqualify the text of the letter, the relationship with his wife and son, and avoid any definition of his relationship with the therapists. Furthermore, by severely disciplining Bruno in the session, he was denying any coalition with the child, a coalition which had been alluded to in the letter.

We can therefore observe how the dominant communicational mode in the session was the disconfirmation of self and of the other in the relationship. This is more than evident in the behavior of Jolanda. As a matter of fact, Jolanda really did not exist in the relationship, neither with her son nor with her husband. She was with her own family (her parents) when she suffered, and with Doctor Selvini when she loved and hoped.

The disconfirmation of self in his relationship with his wife and son was less dramatic in Luigi, perhaps less fanciful, but just as fundamental. He did not resort to Jolanda's maneuver, which interposed between husband and wife people to hate (her parents and brother) or people to love (Doctor Selvini), so that she could avoid declaring whether she hated or loved him, Luigi, or if she expected some concrete statement from him. Luigi did not react to this maneuver, as it worked out very well for him. (It was as if Jolanda were saying: "Now, between us there's a new person. Doctor Selvini. She might disappoint me, but *you can't*, since I'm asking nothing from you, or at the most, impossible things.")

Luigi, for his part, claimed to accept the therapists' definition of his character: a weakling. But this acceptance was nothing other than a disqualification, since in the text of the letter, Luigi was *not* defined as a weakling, but as a person considered to be such by his son in his relationship with his wife. Luigi in fact disqualified even this disqualification by his manner, through his tone of voice, gestures, and the shrugging of his shoulders. He admitted to having been anxious, but this was only because of Jolanda's sudden and overwhelming reaction to the flashback of her childhood. Thus, even Luigi did not exist, in any relationship, not even in that with the therapists, toward whom he refused to express any feelings. On the basis of this observation, the therapists decided to make an intervention which would attack the central problem, that is, the impossibility in the couple to make a definition of the relationship. It was urgent that we find a therapeutic paradox. We decided to give the couple a written prescription, in which a clear and identical definition would be made of their relationship, placing both husband and wife on the same level. Their relationship would be arbitrarily defined as one of love, which, being intolerable for the partner, has to be denied or disconfirmed. Since the principal weapon used by both members of the couple was disconfirmation, we would prescribe the disconfirmation, being careful to connote it positively. The end of the session follows:

The two therapists reentered the therapeutic room, having decided that Doctor Selvini was to conclude the session and make the prescription.

Female therapist: "All of us in the team have been impressed by the deep love that ties the two of you together. [pause] But we were even more impressed by the danger that that love may come to the fore."

Jolanda (in a deep voice): "That's true...."

Female therapist: "And how were we able to understand this?

[pause] By realizing that in our last session we made a serious mistake. By giving you that letter to read, in which, for the first time, there were no outsiders, but only the four of you, we increased the danger that that love could declare itself, which could only cause you grief and suffering, as we saw today. It's very important that we correct that mistake, and to do that, we're going to give you another prescription. Here are two sheets to read, one for you, Jolanda, and the other for you, Luigi. Since today is Wednesday, each of you will read his sheet to the other each Wednesday evening before going to bed, until our next session, which will be after the summer holidays. We say this about a next session, because we have decided to offer you a second series of ten sessions, which will begin August 31. That is, of course, if you agree with us.

Jolanda (immediately): "Thank you!"

On Jolanda's sheet, which was to be read first, was the following:

Luigi,
  I do not see you, I don't hear you, because I'm not even here, I'm with Doctor Selvini. I'm doing this for you, because if I were to show you how much I love you, I would put you in an intolerable position.

On Luigi's sheet was the following:

Jolanda,
  I can't say that I have hostile feelings for Doctor Selvini because, even if I did, and if I said so, it would be the same as saying I love you, and this would put you in an intolerable position.[26]

After having read the text aloud, the couple remained immobile, as if paralyzed. The two children, also immobile and alert, watched them intently. While Bruno seemed embarrassed, Chicco looked from one to the other, with his mouth half-open, as if in shock. No one said anything, and the two therapists rose and left.

In the subsequent team discussion the observed feedbacks were analyzed. We had some doubts about the correctness of declaring that what we had said in the first written text was an error. We concluded we had been correct. This resulted from the analysis of the data.

In the first written text we made the move of defining the nuclear family as something separate from the extended family with its own problems of relationship. The response of the family was a countermove of disqualification of all parts of the message: the introduction of an outsider in the relationship (female therapist), a flashback to the past with the extended family, and the disconfirmation of the spouses as nonexisting in the relationship. Such countermoves of the family suggested to us the new intervention. We accepted the disqualification upon declaring as an error our attempt to define the nuclear family as separate from the extended one.

With the second written message, we had adopted the family game. We had introduced an outsider, the female therapist, positively connoting and prescribing the inability of the spouses to face each other and to define the relationship. But, in doing this, we had also clearly (though arbitrarily) defined their reciprocal relationship as one of love, metacommunicating on the rule of the game: the clear definition of the relationship is intolerable.

Thus, husband and wife found themselves on the same level, both losers in the same game, which was the only real winner.

This detailed description of the therapeutic interaction can clarify and illustrate what was said in the beginning of this chapter. In fact, the reader who considered "playing schizophrenic as coldly as possible" to be a cynical attitude toward suffering will now understand that we are fighting against the *game,* and not against its *victims.*

chapter 15

THE PROBLEM OF SECRET COALITIONS

Another constant phenomenon observed by researchers in the dysfunctional family is the presence of perverse coalitions which perpetuate the battle between opposing factions. Many authors have touched on the subject, but it was Jay Haley who described with the greatest clarity its essential characteristic in a conference held in 1964, later published under the title "Toward a Theory of Pathological Systems" (1966). In this work Haley brilliantly distinguished between *declared alliances for* (something) and *denied colations against* (somebody). The latter he labeled "perverse triangles." Haley says:

1. The people responding to each other in the triangle are not peers, but of different generations. By "generation" we mean a different order in the power hierarchy, as in a human generation of parent and child or in an administrative hierarchy such as manager and employee.
2. In the process of their interaction together, the person of one generation forms a coalition with the person of another generation against his peer. By "coalition" is meant a process of joint action which is *against* the third person (in contrast to an alliance in which two people might get together in a common interest independent of the third person).

3. The coalition between the two persons is denied. That
   is, there is certain behavior which indicates a coalition
   which, when it is queried, is denied as a coalition. More
   formally, the behavior at one level which indicates that
   there is a coalition is qualified by metacommunicative
   behavior indicating there is not.

Regarding this distinction (Haley 1966, pp. 16-17) between
alliances-for and coalitions-against, experience has shown us
that an intergenerational alliance inside a family may be, in
many cases, not only possible, but sane. Such is the case of the
father who, in the presence of an overanxious wife, *allies himself
openly* with the adolescent son *for* the purpose of facilitating his
autonomy, at the same time helping his wife to accept the
changed situation.

With the growth of our experience and observational
capacity, we have noted the constant presence of a certain level
of confusion in the intergenerational boundaries (excessive
parentification—Boszormenyi-Nagy and Sparks 1973, p. 151)
of some member of the second generation, a reciprocal
seductivity in the relationship between one of the parents and
one of the children, coalitions and factions more or less open in
all the disturbed families which present a nonpsychotic
patient. In one of our families presenting a neurotic adolescent,
we experienced something very close to embarrassment when
we observed the open and continual looks of passionate love
exchanged between mother and son. In families presenting
anorectic patients, the observation of redundancies indicating
intergenerational intricacies is already more difficult due to
the contradictions and denials (Selvini Palazzoli 1973, p. 202).

It is with the families we are speaking of in this book that
these difficulties reach their extreme height. The reader who
has followed us in the previous chapters will have, we believe, a
clear and dramatic idea of the inexhaustable store of denials,
contradictions, omissions, pseudo-revelations, disqualifications, derailments, smoke screens, sabotages, etc. kept ever
ready in the incredible armory of these families for the purpose
of misleading.

For a certain period of time in our research, we believed we had found a rule: the exhibition of opposites. We believed that the secret coalition accompanied by an exhibition of hostility and violence was the key to our research. But even this path, if at times useful, proved simplistic. We had, therefore, to go ahead gradually with great care, using progressive interventions suggested by feedbacks obtained step by step. But as the "problem" we were searching for revealed itself—a hidden coalition, for example, between the father and the identified patient against the mother, often with allusive erotic hints— the position in which we put ourselves became fundamental: that of not concerning ourselves with the problem's "reality" in the intrapsychic sense. The "problem" should be considered only as a move, undoubtedly central, in the formation and maintenance of the game. Considering it an intrapsychic "reality" brings one to search for the *cause*, the *reasons* to be concerned with the suffering and gratifications experienced by the individual members. All this results not only in an enormous loss of time, but in entering a labyrinth with little probability of exit.

Causes, reasons, and feelings should all remain in Pandora's box, as it were. This does not mean that we therapists, having a psychoanalytic formation as we do, do not regularly discuss the session using the linear and psychoanalytic model, punctuating and formulating causal hypotheses giving ourselves historical explanations, confronting them with those of our colleagues in the team discussion. This is inevitable, as it is inevitable that we make use of language. All the same, in the moment in which we attempt to formulate a therapeutic intervention, we force ourselves to transcend language, considering what we see in the circularity of its here and now, as the pivot, the nodal point of the momentary equilibrium of the opposing factions.

Once we have grasped the nodal point, we find ourselves at the crucial moment, that of the intervention.

In order to provoke changes which are therapeutic, this intervention should be rigorously global and systemic. It should involve the entire family, avoiding any moralistic division between the individual and various members or factions. The therapists metacommunicate on the coalitions and connote them positively for their good and affectionate aims. Such coalitions, however, are not explicitly prescribed. Moreover, the comment is elaborated in such a way as to become intolerably paradoxical.

So that the reader might have a clear idea of this tactic, it is indispensable to give examples. It is well known how difficult and frustrating it is to put an individual therapy into words. We find it even more difficult to do so with a family therapy; it is often impossible to express that atmosphere of tension, with its continuous and circular actions and feedbacks occurring simultaneously on various levels, whose nonverbal components (gestures, postures, tones of voice, glances, and facial expressions) are the most important vectors of meaning.

Once more the linear and discursive model betrays us. We have to resign ourselves to the closest approximation, since "it is impossible," as Shands notes, "to describe circular patterning precisely because the nature of *symbolic* operations is different from the nature of physiological operations. Naively, it is easier to distort observations so as to reinforce the notion of linearity than it is to cope with the ambiguity implicit in circular physiological patterning....Describing physiological processes in linear discursive terms appears somewhat like squaring a circle—at best, the result is an approximation" (1971, p. 35). Thus, after the effort of giving an example, we find ourselves with something colorless, watered down, so undramatic as to make us think "but...was that all?..." All the same, we will continue this effort of offering approximations, since we cannot do otherwise. Therefore, with the awareness of our handicaps, we offer to the reader the following case.

The Aldrighi family (a family of seven members) was sent to us because of their daughter Sofia, who, at the age of nineteen had developed delusional ideas and psychotic behaviors. When the family therapy began, Sofia was twenty-two years old and had been under pharmacological treatment as well as in individual psychotherapy, with no apparent results.

The communicational mode of the family, in the first session, had revealed an interesting phenomenon: although we were dealing with a family of the middle class, well-educated and cultured, conversation was difficult due to many strange expressions, a peculiar way of pronouncing certain words, and the tendency to leave sentences unfinished. While the therapists found themselves in great difficulty, the family had the air of understanding everything perfectly. Without commenting on this phenomenon, the therapists limited themselves to asking every once in a while the repetition of a word or phrase, until the family happily explained that it possessed a sort of private language. From their habit of talking a lot and all together, especially when talking to the mother, they had acquired the habit of abbreviating, of using hints and slogans in order to understand each other all the more quickly.

A second important observation was that of the reluctance shown by the family, and especially by the mother, to speak of Sofia's "symptoms." It was as if this subject were a holy secret and speaking of it would be indelicate. Everyone showed a kind of bashful respect for Sofia.

The intervention we wish to describe took place in the eighth session, after a series of other paradoxical interventions which had provoked important changes in the younger generation. The oldest son, who had for years sustained the role of go-between for his parents, had recently left home but continued to come to the sessions. A daughter, Lina, in whom we had perceived the temptation of voluntarily assuming the place left vacant by her brother, had renounced it following its paradoxical prescription by the therapists in the fifth session. The mother, who had initially been vivacious and talkative, seemed depressed, tired out, and was visibly aged (as if the departure of her son and the new behavior of Lina had deteriorated her).

Sofia, for her part, had emphasized certain aspects of her psychotic behavior. From the very beginning she had come to the sessions dressed in shabby masculine clothing, close-cropped hair, unpolished and worn-down shoes, and different colored socks. In the first session she had signaled her absence by sinking down into her chair and raising the collar of her sweater so that it covered her face and ears. Later, abandoning this behavior, she had spent the time during the sessions by writing mysteriously in a small, greasy notebook, responding when spoken to, with phrases reminiscent of the Pythian enigma, which the family (but not the therapists) tried in vain and in awe to decipher. From the corner of her eyes she kept the whole group under constant observation, especially the female therapist, to whom she exhibited a kind of sarcastic respect, jumping to her feet to pass her an ashtray, or opening the door for her with a stiff bow and a click of the heels, as if she were a recruit saluting the passage of a general.

In the eighth session, after the above-mentioned changes in the family, she presented herself even more shabby and mannish than ever. The family told us unhappily that Sofia, who for some time had had the habit of cursing to herself, had done so all during the train trip to Milan, making the passengers in their compartment leave. These curses had been in relation to a rash which for several weeks she had had under the armpits and around the anus. During the session, Sofia got up frequently to scratch herself in the affected zones, quite in the manner of a he-man truck driver. Furthermore, she had, according to the family, become more unpredictable than ever, having "completely lost all sense of time." She paid no attention to the hour, staying out until late at night, upsetting the family's schedule for meals, etc. At other times she refused to move from home, cursing for hours, and there was no way to get her to go out. They found this last behavior extremely embarrassing when her sisters' boyfriends came to visit. As a result of this behavior, Lina said during the session, she would like to get away for two weeks to stay with a girlfriend and study for some exams. At home, some of her tasks would be taken care of by her brother, who would return during her absence. This project, she added, would only be carried out with the eventual permission of the therapists.

In the discussion following the session, the two observers offered a hypothesis which was immediately shared by the two therapists. Sofia was effectively miming a sort of imaginary father, impervious, ancestral, authoritarian, and vulgar. With this behavior she was communicating to everyone how dangerous it was, in a family in which everyone wished to escape, to have a "weak and ineffectual father," such as the very gentlemanly Mr. Aldrighi, and how extremely important it was that someone take his place, especially in the control of "the women."

The intervention for the conclusion of the session, minutely discussed and prepared by the team, was to be carried out by the male therapist as follows:

Male therapist: "Our team believes that the Aldrighi family, as we see it today, has no need for a father different than the one it already has. [pause] But we have Sofia, who has put it in her head the family needs a completely different father: an old-fashioned kind of father, who keeps the women quiet, who controls them, who isn't influenced by their demands, and who comes and goes as he pleases without any time limits. He's a father who doesn't try to be subtle or pleasant, who doesn't bother with good manners, who doesn't hold back with curses and insults, and if he has to, he'll scratch his behind when he wants to. Sofia is honestly convinced that the family needs this kind of father, and has taken it upon herself to take up the role. For this, she is generously sacrificing her youth and her femininity. Instead, she worries about the femininity of her sisters, controlling them in the way of olden-day fathers, so that they will not make any false steps."

Lina (interrupting): "Aha! That's why she is always on top of me when Francesco comes! Now I understand. And if I kiss him!...She gives me these looks....Instead she leaves my brother alone when he's with his fiancée."

Male therapist: "That's what ancestral fathers always did. But let's go on with our conclusion. As I have already said, we therapists do not agree with Sofia's conviction, but are unanimous in respecting it because it's an honest conviction, and she's paying personally for it. Therefore, in respect to the request of Lina, you have to ask Sofia. From now on, you should ask permission from her for everything."

Lina: "...but, I...then...what should I do? Obey Sofia?..."

Male therapist: "We can't give you any advice, Lina. If we did, we would be contradicting ourselves. We respect Sofia's honest conviction that she should represent the paternal authority in the family."

Father (heatedly, turning to Lina): "So then, organize yourself accordingly. What would you do with a father like that? What would you do if I were like that? Adjust yourself, right? You can even rebel if you want to!"

In the meantime, Sofia, in her chair, intently chewing her nails, did not once open her mouth. When the therapists left the room, she did not rise to open the door for the female therapist as was her ritual.

In the discussion following the session, we predicted great changes in the organization of the family game. It seemed inevitable that Sofia would change, abandoning her sisters to their own fates. We discussed the worn-out air of the mother and her silence, as well as the heated utterances of the father, whom we believed to have been encouraged by the intervention of the male therapist. It is worth noting that everyone in the family had been impressed by the passivity of the female therapist, who had limited herself to listening with respect and agreement to the comment of her colleague. More than one of them had tried to get her involved in the discussion, but we had already agreed among ourselves that she would behave in this way, especially since the family had already often enticed her into a dominant role in previous sessions, thereby repeating the family game.

The eighth session took place just before the summer holidays, and two months passed before the ninth session was held. The family presented itself punctually, all members being present. The eldest brother announced himself married, while Lina, who had graduated with excellent grades, had passed most of the vacation with friends. Sofia, by contrast, had remained, with two of her younger siblings, with her parents in a rented house at the seashore. We were hardly able to recognize her. Attractive, although without make-up, with her hair curled and brushed, she was wearing a long flowered dress and fashionable sandals.

The seating of the family during this session offered us an immediate observation. The mother sat by herself in the row of chairs in front of the mirror. The seats on either side of her were empty. On the left, in respect to the mirror, was Sofia, with her father at her side, for the first time. On the other side, in a group, were the other siblings. After giving us the information about their summer, the father launched into an invective on the behavior of Sofia. "If I compare this summer to last summer, I have to say that things are much worse! Sofia tortures my wife to the point that I fear for her health. If I don't commit her, I'll have to send my wife to a hospital! Our vacation was a hell!"

The mother said nothing during this tirade and, except for the sad expression on her face, seemed in better physical shape than ever: she had gained some weight, was tanned and elegantly dressed.

After his lament, the father, as if unable to go on so close to Sofia, rose suddenly and seated himself in the last empty seat near the group formed by the other children, using his need of an ashtray as an excuse, although there had been one right next to this original seat. The therapists, as usual, made no comment.

Once their father was among them, Sofia's brothers and sisters, each in turn, began a diatribe against her. They accused her of not really being crazy, since her behavior was reserved for the benefit of her family, while outside the house she behaved properly (even nicely!) to the point of their receiving compliments about her (this fact, not previously mentioned by the father, came out in the course of the rather heated conversation). They accused her of not studying, of not working, of making the family support and maintain her. Incredible, her, with all her revolutionary ideas against the bourgeois family! "Why don't you get out once and for all!" shouted one of her sisters, "and leave Mother in peace! But Mother would have to kick you out instead of being your servant! Since you're not crazy you should get out!"

At this point the father interrupted, saying that Sofia was crazier than ever, and he had never been so sure of it. She was (in his words) completely incapable of taking care of herself.

During all this uproar, the mother did not react but smoked

in silence. When asked by the therapists what she thought of
Sofia, she replied with gentle denials and contradictions. She
disqualified the children by saying that she was not worried
about Sofia. She disqualified her husband by saying that Sofia
could leave and take care of herself very well. But it wasn't up
to her to impose this decision on Sofia, for then it wouldn't be
Sofia's decision. She immediately contradicted herself by saying
that she always had to think about the girl because of her total
unpredictableness. Before ever saying anything, she always
had to ask herself if she was saying the right or wrong thing.
She was happy the rare times she was able to do or say the
right thing! What else could a mother do?

During the long diatribe of her brothers and sisters, Sofia,
contrary to her usual attitude, had faced her accusers,
provoking them with cutting criticisms, exasperating them
with political digressions, inviting them to do as she did, that is,
not to care about her at all! During her mother's comments,
however, she remained silent, feigning an air of superiority.

Finally, since the session had carried on over the hour, one of
the therapists closed the session by turning to the youngest
son, a ten-year-old who had always remained silent, although
visibly attentive. He was asked what his impression had been,
during the summer, of his parents, how he had seen them
together. "Worse than last year," the boy answered immediately, "when Sofia was sick. This year they were a lot more
anxious and nervous with each other. Daddy was mad at
Mamma when she kept dinner hot for Sofia when Sofia was
out late. Mom was unhappy. Papa and Celia [a sister] talked
with Mom for hours, trying to make her promise, if Sofia was
late, not to save her dinner, not to ask any questions. And then
Papa would get furious when Mama broke her promise..."

The mother (meekly): "I always did what you wanted me to do.
I'm sure....Maybe once or twice, I don't really remember."
(Indignant chorus from the family and exit of the therapists.)

In the team discussion, we tried to make a summary of the
phenomena we had observed. Sofia had reacted to the
preceding prescription by abandoning the role of ancestral
father and by presenting herself in very feminine clothing. Her

behavior during the session was no longer psychotic. From the description of her behavior during the summer, we gathered that she had secretly become allied to her mother, hiding this coalition behind a facade of insults and "tortures." The mother, for her part, hid her own alliance with Sofia behind her anxiety and servility, which were acceptable in a "good mother."

This privileged twosome threatened the others of the family, inciting them to impotent fury. In fact, it was evident that Sofia and her mother felt themselves in a position of power and superiority. We had to find a comment that would paradoxically upset the entire family epistemology, that would put *all* the members of the family in an unsustainable position, thus forcing them to change.

Since this was a crucial moment, we decided to make a written prescription. This would introduce an unexpected and dramatic element in the therapy. The therapists would tell the family of their decision to write down the prescription, and ask the father to have photocopies of the prescription made so that each member would have his own. The therapists were to read the prescription aloud, while their colleagues behind the mirror would attentively watch the various reactions in the family. The comment was as follows:

> We have been profoundly moved by the action shared by Father, Antonio, Lina, Celia, and Renzino to encourage Sofia to fill Mother's life. In fact, they have the conviction that someone in the family, taking turns, should always keep alive Mother's interest, even if this makes her suffer. Thus, knowing Sofia's independent spirit very well, they realize that the more they insist that she leave Mother, the more they force her to attach herself to Mother.

The silence that followed the reading of the comment was absolute. Everyone, as if nailed to their seats, stared at us without moving an inch. The therapists rose to give the prescription to the father, at the same time stating the date of the next session. While the others slowly got to their feet, the mother remained rigid in her seat. Sofia said good-bye to the therapists, offering a limp hand and a tense smile, in an attempt to show herself as being up to the situation.

The intervention described here should make the definition we gave at the beginning of this chapter more understandable. It was strictly global, systemic, and included all members of the family, with no exception. Any moralistic distinctions between the various members and the various factions were avoided.

The denied coalition "Mother-Sofia," demonstrated in an allusive manner, was placed on the same level as the open coalition "Father–other children." The attitude of the latter, far from being connoted negatively as jealous competition, was connoted positively as solicitude and affection toward the mother. Such a comment was upsetting to everyone, especially Sofia. What on earth could a girl do, when she had been defined by the therapists as independent to the point of being *obliged* by others *to be* dependent in order to be able to *believe* herself independent??

chapter 16

THE THERAPISTS DECLARE THEIR IMPOTENCE
WITHOUT BLAMING ANYONE

The therapeutic interventions so far presented are all of the active and prescriptive type. Our experience has shown us, however, that it is indispensable to include in the therapeutic armamentarium an intervention which is apparently the exact opposite and, as we shall see, paradoxical: the declaration by the therapists of their impotence.

As we have seen, some families respond to interventions with progressive changes, while others, who at the moment seem to be struck, return to the successive sessions completely unchanged, and, in fact, more than ever entrenched in their family game. They have either disqualified or "forgotten" the comments of the therapists, or have succeeded in finding some other way of escaping an apparently well-directed intervention. The resulting disappointment of such a reaction stimulates the therapists to become all the more zealous in the effort to invent more and more powerful interventions, while the family continues to disqualify them.

Thus begins an unending game in which it is impossible to decide whether it has been the family that has enticed the therapists into a symmetrical escalation, or rather the zeal or hubris of the therapists themselves.

At this point, persistence would only increase the escalation and the only weapon left to the therapists is a change in their position in the relationship, that is, in the definition of the relationship, by honestly declaring their impotence. However, it is important that in making this declaration the therapists avoid any blame of the family; this would be the same as making an extreme and miserable attempt to define themselves as "superior." In order to avoid this, it is very important to prepare not only the verbal content of the declaration but, above all, to control their nonverbal attitude, which might easily reveal vexation, irony, or accusation.

In fact, we say that in spite of the willing collaboration of the family, which has done everything possible to facilitate our understanding, we find ourselves confused and incapable of forming clear ideas, of helping them, and that the team discussion has in no way clarified our ideas. The attitude of the therapists should be neither indifferent nor overdramatic but simply that of those who dislike acknowledging their incapacity in doing what has been asked of them.

In saying this, we attentively observe the various feedbacks of the members of the family. We leave a pause of "suspense," fix the date for the family's next session, and collect our fee.

A behavior of this type always makes a great impression on our families, which have become accustomed to receiving a comment or prescription at the end of every session. The immediate reaction is always one of astonishment, often followed by intense agitation and requests for help. The fear of losing their "adversaries" forces the family to do something, anything, to keep the game going—"so...then, what about us, what can we do?"—and often brings them to the point of making a generous self-accusation: "But couldn't it all be *our* fault?"

To this question, the therapists, in their new position of impotence, have no answer. We really don't know what to say. After this, we reconfirm the date for the next session, without saying that we hope that things will go better next time. This, of course, is left cryptic and unclear, almost like the Damoclean sword hanging over the future of the group. And if things were to become worse?....

As in all therapeutic interventions, the timing of this maneuver is fundamental. It can't be premature. The correct moment occurs, in our experience, when the angry obstinacy of the therapists is a sure sign of escalation, while the family, on its part, reinforces its disqualifications. This occurs most frequently when an intervention has had an effect which has shaken the status quo of the family. In such cases, according to the style of these families, through a shower of the more or less hidden disqualifications, one can glimpse certain premonitions of change which have frightened the family and caused them to react in this way. It is exactly at this moment that it is necessary for the therapists to resist the temptation to insist. It is the right moment to declare themselves impotent.

There are two reasons for such a move. The first has been explained: to break the symmetrical game which has involved both family and therapists. The second, just as important, was discussed in the chapter on positive connotation: the therapists must avoid defining themselves as initiators of change, and therefore as hostile to the family, which will defend to the end its status quo.

This intervention derives its efficacy through the fact that it is paradoxical, and paradoxical on several levels. In fact, while the therapists declare themselves confused and unable to decide what to do, they are in reality accomplishing a great deal: they are defining themselves, in a relationship which has until this moment been symmetric, as complementary.

But in defining themselves as complementary by virtue of their own incapacity, rather than of any fault of the family, they are really *not* being complementary, since they thereby gain control of the situation. Their making the next appointment and collecting the fee communicate a definite professional assurance in complete contrast with the declaration of impotence. Where a real situation of impotence would involve an incongruence in the fixing of any future appointments, here the failure to fix an appointment would be a serious error. It would be the same as making a punitive communication to the family, as well as a depressive statement about ourselves. On the other hand, making an appointment without any critical comment will compel the family, which is quite aware of its sabotage tactics, to come up with something new next time in order to continue the game. That all this is true, we have had demonstrated in the cases where we resorted to this intervention. Seeing their adversaries undernourished and weakened, the family returned to the battlefield offering emergency rations. In these sessions, more "secrets" were revealed than in all the previous sessions combined.

The basic strength of this tactic lies in the fact that it exploits one of the fundamental rules of the family game: never permit the collapse of the enemy. He has to be kept in fighting condition and, in any moment of weakness, should be given encouragement. But this, naturally, with prudence and discretion, and only if the enemy has proved himself worthy of such consideration.

We used this intervention in the case of the Bossi family. In our opinion, this family would *never have been able to change* had the therapist not declared, at the correct moment, her impotence. Here we speak of a single therapist because, toward the end of the therapy, we discovered that the referring doctor had sent the family to our center with the following words: "And remember that I am sending you to Doctor Selvini, a *magician* who doesn't miss a trick. She recently cured a case worse than yours in a single session." Only this last information was true, and the Bossi family, which lived in the area, had heard of the "miracle." Here we cannot resist telling the story of this "miracle," which clearly illustrates the power of a therapeutic paradox which hits the right target.

This case deals with the family of a twelve-year-old anorectic boy, the first case of true anorexia nervosa in a male we had dealt with. In addition to all the typical symptoms, Giulio, the identified patient, spent hours massaging his hips and legs with an expensive slenderizing cream. After the first session, both the boy and the family reacted to a paradoxical intervention made by the therapist (Doctor Selvini) with an immediate and radical change in behavior.

This family could be characterized by the social difference between father and mother. The mother was a schoolteacher while the father was a blue-collar worker. He, visibly intimidated by his learned wife, spent his free time playing bocce, a popular game similar to lawn bowling. Traditionally only men participate, drinking wine and cracking jokes. He was a champion at it, and frequently won tournaments and trophies. Giulio was not permitted to follow his father in these outings, which often occurred on Sunday: "Daddy comes back late at night, and Giulio has to get up early and be fresh for school in the morning." Naturally, Giulio was the best student in his class. He spent Sunday afternoons with his mother and eight-year-old brother revising his lessons and taking long walks, during which he was gently instructed in botany and mineralogy.

This information came from the parents, and Giulio, negativistic and hostile, refused to open his mouth. After the team discussion, the female therapist (Dr. Selvini) carried out the following intervention:

I have to excuse myself, Giulio, to your doctor for having doubted his diagnosis. When he told me on the telephone that you had anorexia nervosa I thought: it's impossible, he must be wrong. Anorexia nervosa is a female disease! A male can't have a female disease! And instead, that's exactly what you have, Giulio! But why? [pause] We have talked for more than one hour with your parents and we can't find anything in their behavior that can explain this strange phenomenon. [pause] Our only explanation is that there has been some kind of misunderstanding. That perhaps you've got the idea that in teaching you, in expecting obedience, good manners, good work in school, respect toward your grandparents, in expecting you to keep away from foulmouthed boys, your parents wanted a Giulietta instead of Giulio [clamorous laughter on the part of the brother, followed by a progressive, moving lightening of Giulio's face, finally bursting out in uncontrollable laughter, while the parents, embarrassed, seemed to hold their breaths] But things cannot be like this. [raising the tone] Daddy and Mommy can only want that you become a man, a real man [sounds of agreement from the parents]. [pause] Anyway, at this point, if this is your conviction, that in order to become a man you need a woman's disease, we agree with the path you have chosen. We respect it. Not only do we respect it, but we think you should continue to be anorectic. And to you, parents, we recommend the same things: this feminine disease should continue, because Giulio is convinced that only with a feminine disease can he become masculine.

When the family presented itself at the second session, Giulio had gained several pounds. We were told that, on their trip home from the first session, the family had stopped in a restaurant. When the waiter had come, Giulio had immediately ordered for himself: "Bring me spaghetti," which he devoured under the astonished eyes of his parents. He had changed not only in his eating habits, but also in other things. He had become disobedient at school, did only what was minimally necessary, had begun to play bocce, and attended a gym for wrestling. But many other things had changed as well. The parents, evidently terrorized by that "feminine" emphasized in the comment, not only permitted him these sports activities but had organized parties at home to which they invited his peers. The therapy continued for another four sessions, and ended with a fit and proud Giulio, who had just won a junior cup in bocce.[27]

Returning to the Bossi family, the unfortunate recommendation of the referring doctor, made in this case to a family characterized by a typical schizophrenic game, could only sound to them like an exciting challenge.

The first session was characterized by an almost intolerable meaningless chatter. The family was made up of five members, the parents and three children, the identified patient, Agnese, being the middle child. Fourteen years old, and anorectic for more than two years, she had complicated the initial symptomatology with psychotic behavior and delusions. To describe fully the stormy therapy of this family one could write an entire volume, which would have to be accompanied by films and tape recordings of the team discussions. Here we shall say only that we tried everything, all the interventions so far described in this book, to no avail. We even reached the point of having to double the agreed upon number of sessions with a second series of ten sessions, regardless of the great distance the family had to travel to come to our center in Milan. For them, the excitement of the "match" must have been worth every moment of discomfort.

The family responded to our various interventions with a variety of brilliant disqualifications, while Agnese, for her part, passed from extreme thinness to a flaccid obesity, reinforcing at the same time her psychotic behavior. All the same, the family continued to come!

When by the seventeenth session we had reached a state of total exasperation, we finally understood the absolute need of declaring ourselves impotent without placing the blame on anyone. We hypothesized that the family challenge had concentrated on the female therapist, since she was considered an authority in the field of anorexia. We decided, therefore, that she was the one who should humiliate herself in front of the family by declaring her own impotence. The parents reacted to this move with amazement and fright. But on the face of Agnese we were able to observe a smile of satisfaction as she rose from her chair to gather her coat and sweater. This smile was the first sign that we had finally made the right move.

The next session, which occurred a month later, was memorable. The discussion was opened by the father, who described how much Agnese had improved in the last few weeks. She ate more regularly, no longer made scenes at mealtime, and ate more than usual. She was on friendly terms with her older sister (after years of hostilities) and had made new friends. To this information, he added a half-dozen family "secrets." Having unexpectedly become intelligent and psychologically sophisticated (he had up to now maintained the role almost of a moron), he began to offer certain crucial information concerning the evolution of the intrafamiliar relations. The therapists, pleased with this change, temporarily accepted the baited hook. At this point the mother said that Agnese (seated next to her like a statue) had come to this session unwillingly. She had, she said, in cleaning Agnese's room found (by chance!) her diary, of which she had read the last few pages. She had brought it to the session. Could she read it aloud?[28] Agnese, nodding, consented to this, as did the therapists. These pages of the diary resounded in the room like a lamentation of the bitter disillusionment Agnese had experienced at the hands of "Doctor Silvini" (sic, as a reinforcement of the disqualification).

> I asked my parents long ago to bring me to her, and I trusted her. It didn't seem true that I could find myself with a doctor that everyone said was so great, who had cured so many people who had gone to her for anorexia [at this point the mother interrupted her reading in order to tell us of the unfortunate comment of the referring doctor]. Anorexia, what an ugly word! And I, who hoped to free myself from that torment! And instead I made a bigger mistake than ever. Poor me!!

The diary ended with the firm decision to change without any help, to find, like her older sister, a boyfriend and send to hell both psychiatry and psychiatrists.

The diary, read by the mother in a sad tone of voice, was listened to by the therapists with compunction and signs of agreement. Immediately afterward, they left to discuss the case with the team. The two observers remained at the mirror to note the reaction of the various members. The father exclaimed, "We've said and understood more in this session than in all the others put together!" which was greeted by an impatient exclamation from Agnese: "The same old things that don't help me at all." This convinced us, in the team discussion, to insist upon the path we had chosen, that is, of our declaration of impotence in regard to the family. It was therefore necessary to ignore the "positive" change in the behavior of the father and valorize exclusively the diary of Agnese.

Rejoining the family, the female therapist communicated that the only crucial point of the session had been the diary.

She asked Agnese, if she had no objection, to copy out the pages which had been read aloud, and to send them to the center so that she could meditate on them. Agnese agreed to this and a few days later we received the copy of the diary transcribed (by chance!) on paper bearing her father's letterhead. We were certain that, having reached this point, any transformation could occur only over the ashes of the "magician."

chapter 17

THE THERAPISTS PRESCRIBE TO THEMSELVES
THE ULTIMATE PARADOX

As we have shown in chapter 4, the extreme paradox used in the hidden escalation of schizophrenic transaction consists of the following message: "you can only help me by not being what you are."[29] To undermine such a paradoxical request, we devised two counterparadoxes.

The first consists of isolating this paradoxical request from the mass of confusing communicational maneuvers and positively connoting it as right and legitimate.

The second consists of the prescription, applied exclusively to ourselves, to comply with such a request. In this move, however, we are careful to keep one up by making the statement that the continuation and result of the therapy depends almost entirely on our success in putting into effect this self-prescription.

The following example, the eleventh session of a family with a seven-year-old child diagnosed as autistic, will illustrate more clearly these therapeutic moves.

Since the very first session, we had found ourselves continually blocked by the persistent behavior of the young mother, Matilde. An avid reader of books concerning psychoanalysis and the veteran of an unsuccessful analytic therapy, she tended to monopolize the sessions, presenting herself in the role of *the patient in psychoanalytic treatment.*

Between tears and crisis, she kept repeating her past suffering. How miserable her childhood had been and how unhappy her adolescence because of the incomprehension, unfairness, and psychological violence of her parents! Constantly overwhelmed by the memory of these painful experiences, she could not be her real self. What she could have been with a different past!

The attempts of the therapists to change the subject were usually fruitless. The eleventh session, which we shall now recount, was no exception. This time, however (following a therapeutic intervention which had provoked some change in Dedo, the designated patient), her lamentations were so frantic that they clearly revealed their goal: maintenance of the status quo.[30] The therapists were able to pick out, in the confused lamentations of Matilde, some salient points:

a. Matilde, imprisoned as she was in her past, would "get better" only if her past were to *change*.

b. Her husband, Sergio, and her son, Dedo, were urged to cooperate with her in the task of changing her past.

c. The therapists also were urged to do the same, but, even if they were trying, they did not really help her.

d. In fact, the male therapist could help her only if he were to succeed in being her mother, as she wanted her mother to have been. At the same time, the female therapist could only help her if she were to succeed in being her father, but different from her father. But, alas, the therapists had not been able to make it. In fact, the female therapist seemed to her to be severe, as her father had been, while the male therapist, in the last session, had not responded to her glance which was begging from him the tenderness one expects from a mother.

e. But also, Sergio and Dedo had not helped her. She would like to take them back into the past, to start all over again, and in a new way.

f. But Sergio always escaped, staying away from home as much as possible. He owed her a lot. He was nothing when he married her, even if he had had a past far better than her own. And he had kept improving at her expense, casting all the burdens on her poor, weak shoulders. Everyone said he had improved after the marriage.

g. With Dedo, inspired by a recent book on therapeutic regression, she was making a concrete attempt to recreate the past. There was a closet at home where she could close herself for an hour each day with Dedo. Crouching on the floor, she would hold him close to her, as if he were an infant still in the womb. Dedo would say: "We are having our session." More recently (after the delivery!!) they had changed the place, and went instead to Dedo's room, where she would put him in bed and lay close to him. One time he sucked one of her fingers which she offered to him. Yes, Dedo was getting better, but he still tormented her, with his incomprehensible urging for her to repeat stories of the past, songs, phrases, and episodes. Again, again, again. He was never satisfied and she always complied to the point of exhaustion.

In the team discussion, the therapists brought out as the most important element in the session, the radical absurdity of the behavior of Matilde with Dedo. On one hand, she declared her desire to change the past and imposed upon Dedo that he return to the past with her in order to change it. On the other hand, she found Dedo's constant curiosity about the past incomprehensible.

The result of these conflicting messages was that Dedo found himself in the classic double bind: he was damned if he refused to regress upon his mother's request, for therapeutic reasons, and damned if *he* decided to return to the past of his own accord. (At the same time the possibility of metacommunication or of leaving the field were obviously options not open to him.) Dedo, double-binded, reacted by putting his mother in her own double bind by his repetitive request: again, again, again. And in this way, she too was damned, no matter what she were to do. She was damned if she did *not* do it (that is, if she refused to repeat the memories of the past), because this would disappoint him, and she was damned if she *did* do it, because she could never do it enough or to his complete satisfaction.[31]

At this point the therapists decided to concentrate their attention on the relationship between Matilde and themselves, leaving aside any comment on the other point.

The therapists decided, therefore, to bring out the paradoxical request of Matilde, connoting it as both fair and legitimate, and to prescribe to themselves the task of satisfying this request. They would add that only in this way could the therapy go on. The transcript of the closing of the session follows:

Male therapist (emphatic): "We have had to have a long discussion before being able to understand the drama of your family. It is the drama of two people, a husband and a wife, who live in two different historical periods. [pause] Sergio lives 90 percent of the time in the present, in 1974, and 10 percent in the past. On the other hand, Matilde lives 90 percent of the time in the past, in the years between 1940 and 1958, and more or less 10 percent in the present. [pause]"

Matilde: "That's true. . . ."

Male therapist: "We have heard Matilde's request for help, to help her live in the present, as she really wishes to do. We have thought about how we could help her in this, and we have decided that there is only one thing to do, and that is to give a prescription to ourselves. *We* have to change the past for Matilde. We have to try to be what her parents were not in the years between 1940 and 1958. This is our task. It's difficult, and we still don't know how to accomplish it. But we will try as best as we can. [decisive tone] It's indispensable for the continuation of the therapy."

Matilde (drawn back, and almost in a position of defense): "Thank you, I knew you were good . . ."

Female therapist (with visible sign of effort and discomfort, almost as if she were talking to herself): "I have to make myself be what your father wasn't. If I can't be that . . . because only *seeming* to be wouldn't be enough . . . it wouldn't serve anything . . . maybe we won't be able to. . . ."

In the twelfth session, the couple appeared quite changed. They argued openly and fiercely. For the first time Sergio did not give in to the arguments of Matilde, who, having abandoned her usual tearful attitude, seemed firm, even bellicose. She shouted in his face that she was sick and tired of sacrificing herself, of suffering. She wanted to live and enjoy her rights. She had allowed herself to be used, and now it was time to cut it out!

In response to the question of the male therapist as to what she had thought of the last session, she answered that she had felt alone, terribly alone. She had realized that she had thrown us off the track, giving us the impression that she was asking for an impossible and absurd thing. How could we be her parents? No, her parents were what they were, they were different people. As for the rest, even if it were possible, she would never ask us to do such a thing, even though she certainly appreciated our generous offer.

Sergio, the husband, informed us that Dedo had considerably improved. He had had a crisis only after his mother had fixed an old music-box which she had used in the past in his worst moments.

In fact, we were able to observe a visible progress in Dedo's behavior. For the first time he intervened, in a benevolently ironic tone, in an argument between his parents. In the moment in which his mother shouted at her husband—"But where do we go from here, hey, where do we go?"—Dedo got up from his chair and strolled around the room with a carefree air: "To take a nice walk together!"

In the team discussion, we verified the effect of the paradoxical autoprescription. Matilde no longer wanted parents any different from those she had had, nor did she want the therapists to take the place of those parents. (The effectiveness of this maneuver was illustrated by the fact that Matilde never again mentioned either the past or her parents. Obviously she had some other maneuver ready in her armory!) The field having been cleared of this psychotic trap, the therapists decided upon a new paradoxical intervention: to declare themselves preoccupied with Matilde's intention not to suffer any longer.

Male therapist: "We are closing this session with a serious preoccupation. We are worried about you, Matilde . . . yes, about you, who have repeatedly expressed your desire to suffer no more. This is a quite understandable wish, we agree, but at this point it is premature and dangerous for you. Your whole life has been based upon a high moral value, the value of suffering, and it has been this suffering that has let you go on in life, resist, and feel worthwhile. If you give up your suffering this abruptly, you might find yourself lost, deprived of existential meanings, and therefore you may find yourself suffering even more. Sergio and Dedo have sensed this danger and they have always tried to make you suffer so that you wouldn't suffer more."[32]

At these words, Matilde remained momentarily shocked. After an abrupt movement of irritation she quickly controlled herself and came out with, "But, then, what should I do with Dedo?"—a trap-question the therapist quickly neutralized with a final paradoxical prescription: "You have to be spontaneous. In fact, you've already explained to us that when you are spontaneous, you feel anxious (Have I done the right thing?) and therefore you suffer. Be spontaneous, Matilde, it's the best solution."

chapter 18

THE THERAPISTS GIVE UP THE PARENTAL ROLE, PARADOXICALLY PRESCRIBING IT TO THE MEMBERS OF THE LAST GENERATION

The confusion and breakdown between the generations and the consequent reversal and blurring of roles between the different generations is a phenomenon already widely dealt with in psychiatric literature. Here we shall present a specific therapeutic paradoxical intervention developed by our team: the paradoxical prescription of the parentification to the member or members of the last generation at a given moment in the family therapy which coincides with the therapists' abdication of the parental role delegated them by the system.

"By definition, parentification implies the subjective distortion of a relationship as if one's partner or even children were his parents" (Boszormenyi-Nagy and Sparks 1973, p. 151). We should note that parentification is a universal and physiological phenomenon, just as asking for help is universal and functional, in that the person of whom the help is asked, whomever he may be, is always seen as the parent in that moment. The parentification of a child may appear pathological upon first consideration, but it may be functional and ego-structuring, depending on the transactional context in which it occurs. This is the case when the messages between parent and child are clear and the respective roles are elastic and interchangeable in accordance with the changes in the situation, thus permitting the child to experiment and to learn the parental role. This experience of behaving and feeling as a parent, which occurs in early childhood as well as in adolescence, is fundamental in the process of socialization and the achievement of self-esteem and is therefore highly gratifying to the child.

Parentification becomes the cause of dysfunction when it occurs in inappropriate situations in a context of ambiguous or incongruous transactions. The highest level of such dysfunction can be observed in the family in schizophrenic transaction where communications are commonly dominated by the double-bind message.

If we can call physiological parentification an open and direct request for help, we can observe dysfunctional parentification in the family in schizophrenic transaction where it is expressed in a series of pseudo-requests expressed through paradoxical messages, which are incongruous at all levels. Each of the parents communicates the following request to the child: Help me, even if it's impossible; be on my side, but don't be against anyone else. Let me help you, me who is trying to be what a real parent should be. Only by being a real parent to me can you be a real son or daughter for me, and so on. With such a request, how can a child possibly define his position in the family? We can see the resulting confusion in the behavior of a ten-year-old psychotic girl, who throughout the earlier family sessions, flitted uncertainly about, from one parent to the other, while they, sitting in extreme opposite corners of the room, described to the therapists the complete harmony in their marriage!

We can well ask what happens in such a family when it enters therapy. All the experience coming from their respective learning contexts creates an enormous expectation toward the therapists, investing them with the parental role.[33] But what kind of expectation? It conforms to the experience they have carried over from their respective families of origin: each of the two hopes to obtain an unconditional preference from the therapists, to become the "favorite." In their families of origin, in fact, (and we have constantly stated this), the ruling tactic was to bind the child through a calculated distribution of disapproval, always accompanied by the allusive and never fulfilled promise that perhaps, someday, if they were to try hard enough, they would obtain total approval and be preferred over all other members of the family.

The predicted maneuver of each member of the couple is the seduction of the therapists (or of one of the therapists, thus causing a division in the therapeutic team), creating a repetition of the family game, in an attempt to gain the desired approval.[34] One of the major tasks of the therapists is to avoid this trap laid by the couple, refusing any moralistic punctuation. We are, in fact, convinced, especially with this type of family, so incredibly complex, that the acceptance, even if only tactical, of a coalition plays exclusively in favor of the resistance to or the breakoff of therapy. Here we summarize our treatment of the type of family described above.

1. The therapists enter the family system as full-right members, owing to their avoidance of a critical attitude. Rather, they approve of and in some cases prescribe the very behavior they have observed in the family, avoiding any judgment or definition of what or who is good or bad. Interest is shown in the relations between the parents and their respective extended families; and the family may react in three ways: with floods of information, endless trivialities, or frozen attitudes and avoidance, stupidity, and amnesia. Whatever the case, conflicts with and factions within the extended families slowly become apparent.

2. Each parent continues his attempts to make a coalition with the therapists with the purpose of differentiating between the good and the bad in the family system.

3. The therapists repulse this maneuver with a countermaneuver, declaring the identified patient to be the real leader, both good and generous, who has sacrificed himself of his own will for what he believes to be the good of the family, or of one or more of its members. The symptoms of the identified patient are thus qualified and approved of as being spontaneous behavior, decreed by his sensitivity and altruism.[35]

4. The parents, in their relationship with the therapists, who are increasingly parentified, immediately become competitive not only with each other, but also with the identified

patient. At the same time, they speak less of their respective families of origin.

5. The identified patient changes in his relationship with his parents from the position of parent to that of sibling, and begins to abandon his symptoms.

6. The parents intensify their respective attempts to create a coalition with the therapists and to receive some preferential judgment.

7. The therapists refuse to make any such statement, and are increasingly parentified.

8. The identified patient abandons his symptoms and takes a more secondary role during the sessions as well as in his home life.

9. If the family consists of more than one child, one of the identified patient's siblings often produces symptoms at this point.

10. The therapists praise this behavior, attributing it to the child's perception of his parents—fear of terminating therapy.

11. The family presents itself with all the children free of symptomatic behavior. The parents, however, escalate their competitive battle in a last attempt to induce the therapist to continue treatment.

12. At this point the therapists abdicate the role of parents, which, until now, they have accepted, and paradoxically prescribe it to the member or members of the last generation.

We can give an example of this last intervention in the case of a family of four members treated in our center. The parents were young, in their thirties. The identified patient, Claudio, eight years old, had been diagnosed as autistic. He had one sister, five-year-old Detta.

The therapy had been initiated with a contract of twenty sessions, and had been in progress for eighteen months and was approaching termination. For several sessions Claudio had been asymptomatic and was doing well at school. In the eighteenth session, the parents spoke of their preoccupation with Detta, who until this point had shown all the signs of being a "healthy and normal" child. For the past month she had "regressed, become disobedient, noisy, disrespectful, making life at home a hell." In fact, we had already noted a striking difference in her behavior during the session. Normally quiet and cooperative, she had continually disturbed the session, having temper tantrums, shouting, asking to be accompanied to the bathroom, teasing Claudio, who, seated at one side of the room, was trying to read a comic book (It wasn't his problem any more!).

During the team discussion it became clear that the recurring redundancy during the session had been the unusual behavior of Detta. We decided to use this observation for the therapeutic intervention by saying that the little girl, seeing that her brother was "healed," had voluntarily assumed the responsibility of presenting her own symptoms in order to prolong the therapy.

When the therapists returned to the family, they found the parents and Claudio seated and Detta standing in front of her chair, with an attentive and expectant expression in her whole manner. The male therapist addressed the parents.

Male therapist: "We've spent a good deal of time discussing the behavior of Detta just now. [at this, the little girl sat down] You spoke to us about it just now, but, in fact, we certainly noticed Detta today. She really cut up on us! In fact, she was almost like Claudio during our first sessions. So, of course we asked ourselves, how come? Why is Detta so naughty, while Claudio is so good? Finally we understood, we understood her sensitivity. The reason for all this is our silence at the end of the last session, our sending you home without making any comment, without telling you our decision: if it's Daddy who is good and Mommy who's bad, or instead if it's Daddy who is bad and Mommy who is good. And Detta understood that both of you come from families in which there was a brother and a sister, one a bit naughty, and the other a bit good, but no one understood which one was which because Grandmother and Grandfather were always fighting ..."

Mother (interrupting): "Ah ... that's why Detta was saying naughty words about you after the last session. I didn't say so before, out of respect for you, I was ashamed to tell you ..."

Male therapist: "That makes it even more clear! Detta thought at the end of the last session that you were disappointed, that you still needed to come here. So she decided to act like this, now that Claudio is all right, so that you would still be able to come here for a long time ... for as much time as it takes to make a decision."

The parents smiled, the mother's eyes were bright. Claudio, apparently disinterested, leafed through his comic book. And Detta? In the few minutes that had passed, she had fallen deeply asleep! She was curled up in her chair, her head resting on its arm, her mouth wide open.

Female therapist: "Look! Now that her mission is completed, she can rest. Little Detta! She did a hard job today, really hard."

In the nineteenth session both Detta and Claudio were calm and relaxed. Claudio was drawing pictures in a notebook throughout the session, and had completed the schoolyear with good grades. Detta had returned to her normal behavior. Everything had been going well until two days before, when the parents had begun to fight again. In describing how this had started, the quarrel exploded again during the session. The husband accused his wife of being "crazy, intolerant, and aggressive," while he was always the one to accept anything for the sake of peace. The wife accused him of always being the "goody-goody" to get everyone on his side, leaving her all the unpleasant things to do. The therapists observed the quarrel in silence, as spectators, taking no part in it.

During the team discussion, we concluded that this behavior was clearly stating a request, "How do you dare to leave us like this? You have helped our children, yes, but you haven't done anything for us. Now you should give *us* therapy, for *our* problems." The danger implied in such a request seems obvious: that of attracting the therapists, already seduced by their own perfectionism and omnipotence, into a game without end, all the more probable in the absence of the children. On the other hand, if the children had so greatly improved in their behavior, some change must have occurred in the relationship between the parents. By their own admission, everything had gone well until just before this session.

Gradually the team became convinced that the therapy should be suspended immediately, fixing the twentieth and last session after a very long interval. As for the intervention to use at this point, the idea began to grow to use a prescription, paradoxical at many levels, which would succeed in avoiding two dangers: (1) the perpetuation of the parentification of the therapists; and (2) the resumption by the children of the parental role.

The intervention at the closing of the session, minutely prepared and agreed upon by the team, was entrusted to the female therapist. Rejoining the family, she addressed the two children directly, asking them to bring their chairs close in front of her, as if she were telling them a story.

Female therapist: "This time I want to talk to you children, to tell you something. Listen to what I say. There is a city, a large city in England that's called London, where there are a lot of theaters. Do you know what they do at a theater, they act in plays..."

Detta: "I know, I know, I saw one!"

Female therapist: "Good. Did you know that at London there is one theater where for the past twenty-two years the actors always act in the same play? They know it all by heart, and they play their parts every day, year after year, and they can never change it! The same thing has happened to your mother and father. Ever since they got married, they have been playing the same part. We heard it here today. Daddy played the part of the good and the healthy one, and Mommy played the part of the bad and the crazy one. [at this, the father tried to laugh, and the mother remained with her head bowed] We doctors have tried in every way possible to help them play different parts, where the father isn't always good and healthy and the mother bad and crazy, but we haven't been able to, not at all. So we have to give up, but we are putting all our hopes in you. We have seen how much you have changed, and because of that, we hope *you* can do something. Who knows, that in time, you won't get some idea of how to help your parents change their parts, since we haven't been able to do anything. We are going to give you a lot of time. We will meet here in a year—to be exact, next year on July 7."

Detta (immediately): "But next year I have to go to school!"

Claudio (chanting): "Schooldays, schooldays, no more baby games now."

Female therapist: "Surely, and you will have a lot to do, and you will learn a lot in school. Let's hope you get some ideas as to how you can help your parents change their parts, since we have not been able to."

The therapists rose and took leave of the family. The children ran happily toward the door. The parents shook hands with the therapists. For the first time they left the room silently, with thoughtful expressions on their faces.

After their departure, the team commented on the observable reactions. The general impression was that the session had gone well, that it had hit upon the fundamental problem of the family and disarmed it through a series of intertwining therapeutic paradoxes. The therapists had abdicated the parental role conferred upon them by the couple, declaring themselves incapable of responding to their expectations, metacommunicating upon the conflictuality of these expectations, and leaving the field. In such a way, they declared this task requested of them impossible to fulfill. At the same time, they asked the children *to accomplish this impossible task in their place.* Such a prescription is doubly paradoxical. The therapists not only were prescribing something which had been proven impossible for them to fulfill, but *were prescribing something which the children had always tried hard to do.* The children had reacted to this explicit prescription by refusing the task, and leaving the field ("I have to go to school!") The parents were struck by this turning of the tables. They were the only parents left in sight, there were no other parents than themselves!

Thus, the refusal of the therapists to maintain the role of parents in the therapeutic situation is not to be seen as a refusal, but as a *confirmation of the parents,* in that they should be parents, and are certainly able to be. This is so true that the therapists withdraw. We consider this intervention, with the variations required by every case, important in the termination of the family therapy in order to prevent the children from falling again into the parental role when the therapists leave the family system.

In parting, we can add that this intervention is therapeutic for another reason. When the family comes to therapy, the very fact that the parents are requesting help implies a disqualification as parents because they need help. *By abdicating their parental position to the real parents at the correct moment, the therapists validate the parents and confirm them in their natural role.*

Postscript. On July 1, 1976, this family returned for its twentieth and final session. Claudio was a big success in school and a *normal* child in the family—sometimes obedient, sometimes rebellious. The father was no more a "goody-goody" but had assumed a responsible leadership in the family, with the acceptance and cooperation of the wife. The parents were praised for having done all this *by themselves*!

NOTES

1. At the Institute we receive families from all socioeconomic levels. As the reader will see, level of education, I.Q., cultural sophistication, etc. lose their significance as fitness criteria for our type of psychotherapy.

2. Here we use the Greek word *hubris*, which is similar in meaning to the English *pride*. While pride can be healthy, hubris approaches arrogance. It implies a certain superiority and haughtiness, a symmetric tension exaggerated to the point of not giving in in the face of evidence or the very imminence of death.

3. The other day upon the stair,
   I met a man who wasn't there.
   He wasn't there again today,
   Gee! I wish he'd go away!

4. The phenomenon of internal rivals within the group seems to be a constant factor in this type of family. At times, however, a rival external to the group may be invoked. In this case, we are usually dealing with a last desperate step which is meant to threaten the internal rival so that he (or she) will not abandon the field. We have a clear example in the case of the family in which the father on one hand threatens his wife through his tender attachment to his daughter, and on the other hand threatens the daughter by confiding in her his

sexual ties to another woman. The external rival, in this case the father's mistress, whether real or fictional, is introduced as a playing piece in the game so as to prevent the internal rival, that is, the daughter, from leaving the game. Obviously, the variations on this theme are infinite.

5. In such a case (but only in such a case?) love is not for the partner, but rather for the type of interaction with him.

6. In reference to this brusque change from the symmetric to the complementary position in the wolf who receives signs of surrender from the adversary, Konrad Lorenz has hypothesized a special inhibitory effect stimulated by the sign of surrender. Bateson proposes instead the existence of certain possible antithetical codes, one symmetric and the other complementary, which could be represented by two opposing states of the central nervous system. In such a case, the change from symmetry to complementarity would not be the effect of an inhibition, but a sort of global switch into the opposite mental state. The problem arises, however, of how to hypothesize, in terms of the central nervous system, the chronic state of alarm of the members of the family in schizophrenic transaction.

7. It is suggestive to hypothesize also that gamblers ready to ruin themselves at the gaming tables belong to very similar transactional systems. The genius of Dostoyevsky offers astonishing intuitions of this connection in his novels.

8. In Kafka's short novel *The Metamorphosis*, this phenomenon is dramatically portrayed.

9. "Your father Abraham was overjoyed to see my day: he saw it and was glad." The Jews protested: "You are not yet fifty years old. How can you have seen Abraham?" Jesus said: "In very truth I tell you, before Abraham was born, I am."

10. In two families in schizophrenic transaction we discovered that, with the first signs of adolescent crisis in one of the children, a sister rapidly developed a disfiguring obesity accompanied by adolescent fantasies of social success so grandiose and unrealistic that they were destined, given her

physical appearance, to remain only fantasies and therefore guaranteed the status quo. It is very difficult to motivate and keep families with an obese child in therapy, precisely because obesity is neither dangerous to life nor guilt-arousing. It is easy to go to the dietitian or the endocrinologist, so why bother with therapy? In regard to the low-calorie diet, we can observe two tendencies: on the part of the obese patient, a regular inconstancy, and on the part of the family, an incoherent behavior: on the one hand criticizing the patient for her "lack of will," and on the other, stocking the kitchen with goodies and increasing the patient's pocket money. This observation, although limited, confirms the observations made by Hilde Bruch (1957) in the individual treatment of obese youngsters, in whom she discovered frequent thought and communication disturbances of the schizophrenic type.

11. To be exact, we should speak only of countermoves as being observable in the here and now of every system, including the therapeutic one. In fact, even the moves of the therapists are countermoves in response to those made by the family in treatment. According to the cybernetic model, in fact, every member of a system is influenced both by the behavior of the other members of the system and by the effects of his own preceding behavior.

12. As we shall see in the following chapters, such a declaration is an arbitrary reversal of punctuation used by the therapists as an intermediary tactic to start a total change-about of the family epistemology in the systemic direction.

13. Here we mention two notable papers by Harold Searles. In "The Effort to Drive the Other Person Crazy" he accurately describes, already in 1959, the incredible range of tactics used by the schizophrenic patient to seduce his therapist to enter the crazy game. In "Feelings of Guilt in the Psychoanalyst" (1966) he clearly states how the therapist's feelings of guilt are nothing other than the expression of his pretention of omnipotence, exacerbated by his professional training and motivation, as well as by the tactical ability of the schizophrenic patient.

14. As for what has been said in this chapter, the question arises whether a family with the peculiar transactional style we have described must inevitably present, at a certain point in its history, a member behaving in the way usually described as schizophrenic.

For the moment we cannot answer this question; in fact it would take exhaustive longitudinal research, protracted for generations and, unfortunately, made unreliable by many factors, among which are the necessity of funds and cases, the need to adopt a non-eclectic conceptual model and a methodology able to take into account an enormous number of variables, because the family, as we well know, is not an island.

The longitudinal research announced by Riskin, for example, does not seem to respond to these demands, in that the conceptual model he adopted mixes together systemic and linear concepts.

For our part, far as we are from similar projects, we have to limit ourselves to the inverse observation: every family we have treated which presents a member identified as schizophrenic was characterized by the transactional style described above.

15. Here it is important to specify that positive connotation is a metacommunication (in fact, the therapists communicate implicitly about the communication of all the members of the system), and therefore a step up to a superior level of abstraction. Russell's Theory of Logical Types postulates the principle according to which whatever includes all the elements of a collection should not be a term of the collection. In metacommunicating positively, that is, in confirming all the behaviors of the members of the collection, one metacommunicates something about the collection and thereby brings about that step up to a superior level of abstraction (Whitehead and Russell 1910-1913).

16. Here we should point out that the nonverbal aspect of our positive connotation is perfectly coherent to the message: it has no sign of recital, irony, or sarcasm. We are able to succeed in this when we are completely convinced that it is indispensable that we ally ourselves to the here and now of the family's homeostatic tendency.

17. Here we use the word *authority* in the positive sense, as in the latin *auctoritas*, which derives from *augere*—to augment (increase, enlarge) the other in the ontic sense.

18. We formulated this hypothesis with the experience we had gained from earlier cases, most often repeated in families with psychotic children. We often found the parents of these children to be imprisoned in a twofold hidden symmetry: that between themselves, and that with some important member in the extended family, from which each of the two competitively hopes to win the laurels of victory, that is, unconditional approval (which will, of course, never occur).

19. Due to disastrous experiences, we refuse, on principle, to accept a family in therapy as long as any member of that family is in individual therapy. We have seen that in such cases, even if this individual's therapist is in agreement with the family's beginning therapy with us, or is the referring doctor himself, a competitive game unavoidably occurs between the the two therapies.

20. The therapists, in fact, did not point out to the family the repetitive phenomenon they had noticed: if a member of the family risked any criticism of the clan, he was automatically and regularly disqualified by another member of the family. By prescribing the ritual in the manner above described, they succeeded in changing exactly the rule which perpetuated this transactional pattern.

21. Speaking of "crazy games," we can't help mentioning the case of a family of five, the identified patient being Mimma, a ten-year-old psychotic anorectic. She had explained her refusal to eat as stemming from, among other things, a fear of contamination. The family had reacted by transforming the kitchen into a type of operating room where everything was boiled and sterilized. During meals the rest of the family ("anything, just so poor Mimma will eat. Dear God, please make her eat something today!") sat around the table in white lab coats, sterilized gloves and head coverings. Even this

family, when it entered therapy, had no doubts as to who the "crazy" one was—Mimma, of course!

22. We have had concrete proof of the validity of this new approach when three families, with whom we had obtained unsatisfactory results, had the goodness to spontaneously return to us for further treatment. One of these families (with a psychotic patient) did so after an interval of three years, with the not very hidden desire of rubbing our noses in our impotence. Only a few sessions were needed this time in order to change the family game and lead to a transformation.

23. This tactic refers to those absences which occur during therapy, the first session excluded, as it is never given unless all the members of the family are present. In fact, we categorically refuse any attempt made by the parents to have a preliminary meeting with the therapists. After the recording of the preliminary chart following the first telephone contact, the first meeting is always plenary.

24. This reminds us of the frequent case of the preacher in church scolding the attendants for the high number of absentees. Fortunately the devotees do not dare reply: "But Reverend, *we're* here!"

25. This question was a tactical move decided upon beforehand by the team with the intention of obtaining a feedback which could throw light upon the family's game with the therapists. The therapists received the answer without making any comment.

26. At this point the reader may be asking himself not only why families that receive such strange prescriptions follow them, but also why on earth they come to the next session! The fact that they accept the prescription and return to the next session proves once again how the positive connotation, that is, the total acceptance of the family system by the therapists, enables the therapists to be accepted in the family game, where dichotomies such as reasonable) unreasonable, real-unreal, become a false problem, and even more, an impediment to the therapeutic counterplay.

27. Here we repeat our conviction that interventions are strictly specific. A year after the successful conclusion of the case of Giulio, we naively repeated the same intervention in the case of another male anorectic, with an entirely different family situation, without obtaining, as should have been expected, any result.

28. Here is a typical example of the way a family, after an effective intervention, redistributes the roles in order to continue the game. If, this time, the father is the one who is generous with the therapists, someone else will take up the job of disqualifying them.

29. Such a fascinating invitation, certainly not expressed in clear words, must be extrapolated from the mass of communicational maneuvers classically indicated by the term *schizophrenese*. Those psychotherapists who, like ourselves, have had experience in the individual therapy of patients identified as schizophrenic, have certainly experienced the great seductivity of such a message. More than a message, it is an invitation to a total commitment to embark on a marvelous long, long voyage, like that of Ulysses, and like him face the frightening Polyphemus, Circe, and Sirens, as well as the fleeting, if enchanting, Nausicaa. In such a voyage, despite his dedication, the therapist will find himself face to face with his own clumsiness and lack of *real* intuition and *real* sensitivity. How could he have ever expected to be a therapist? He finds himself swept away in a black river of anguish, imprisoned with his patient by insurmountable walls of ice which chill him to the very bone. He finds himself trying to scale the steep walls of a towering pyramid, upon whose apex his patient is stranded, crying out in pain and fear. From time to time, however, he sights the brief hint of a gentle flame which comforts him and leads him to hope once again. Sometimes, like a weary hunter of treasure, he suddenly catches, in the brief light of a flash of lightning, a glimmer of the gems he has so long sought. Sometimes, desperate like a sterile woman, he finds himself carrying in his womb a child eager to be born but is unfortunately unable to give birth to him.

30. Here we have, as noted in chapter 2, an example of the relative length of t_s or time of the system, typical of highly rigid systems. Since the preceding therapeutic intervention, five weeks had already passed. In that period of time, the change of Dedo had alarmed the system. The panic of change had reinforced the corrective maneuver of the mother to the point of making it more clear to the observers. Without a further therapeutic intervention, the system would probably have returned to its status quo. The eleventh session appears, therefore, to have occurred at the right interval to permit the unfolding of two crucial phenomena: the improvement in Dedo and the exasperation of the mother's negative feedback. If the interval had been shorter, for example just one week, there would not have been the time needed for the development of the two related phenomena. In this way, the effects of the therapeutic intervention of the tenth session would have been unobservable because the time elapsed would have been too short compared to the time needed by that system to effect an observable change (t_s). This leads to the hypothesis that, contrary to common practice, the intensity of therapy is not in direct relation to the frequency and total number of sessions.

31. Here the reader may be struck by the similarity with the double bind in which the therapists find themselves in the individual treatment of psychotics. They find themselves between the two binds, of gratification and of frustration.

32. This paradoxical intervention can easily be associated with the Cartesian *Cogito ergo sum*, as "I suffer, therefore I am." This intervention is often successful in dealing with the systemic organizations which have their nodal point in the *martyr-mother*. As we have seen in this case, such a prescription must be systemic, involving all members of the family, martyr as well as "martyrizers," and connoting everyone positively.

33. In most cases, this expectation is secretive and disguised. In some cases, however, it is clearly and insistently shown, with a tendency to disqualify the therapist as being unable to fulfill such a need: "I really thought I could find in *you* a real parent, but what a disappointment so far. But if you try again, who knows?"

34. This maneuver first occurs in the first telephone conversation with the therapist. The caller insinuates his own praiseworthiness: "I'm the good one, your cotherapist, because *I'm* bringing you my family. *I* understand their problem."

35. The "good of the family" varies in every case, and the therapists always base themselves upon concrete information gathered during the therapy.

BIBLIOGRAPHY

Alberti, L.B. (1969). *I Libri della Famiglia*. Torino: Einaudi.

Ashby, W. (1954). *Design for a Brain*. New York: John Wiley.

Ashby, W. (1958). *An Introduction to Cybernetics*. New York: John Wiley.

Bateson, G. (1972). *Steps to an Ecology of Mind*. San Francisco: Chandler Publishing.

Bateson, G., Jackson, D.D., Haley, J., and Weakland, J. H. (1956). Toward a theory of schizophrenia. *Behavioral Science* 1:251-264.

Beels, C.C., and Ferber, A. (1969). Family therapy: a view. *Family Process* 8:280-318.

Bertalanffy, L. von (1968). *General System Theory*. New York: George Braziller.

Boszormenyi-Nagy, I., and Sparks, G. (1973). *The Invisible Loyalties*. New York: Harper and Row.

Bowen, M. (1960). A family concept of schizophrenia. In *The Etiology of Schizophrenia*, ed. D.D. Jackson, New York: Basic Books. Reprinted in M. Bowen, *Family Therapy in Clinical Practice*, pp. 45-69. New York: Jason Aronson, 1978.

Bruch, H. (1957). Weight disturbances and schizophrenic development. *Congress Report of Second International Congress for Psychiatry. vol. 2. Zurich.*

Bruch, H. (1973). *Eating Disorders: Obesity, Anorexia Nervosa and the Person Within*. New York: Basic Books.

Cattabeni, G. (1968). *La Schizofrenia come Espressione della Patologia dell'Organizzazione Familiare.* Thesis at the Psychology Institute of Milan Catholic University, presented by Prof. M. Selvini Palazzoli.

Ferreira, A. J. (1963a). Decision making in normal and pathologic families. *Archives of General Psychiatry* 8:68-73.

Ferreira, A.J. (1963b). Family myth and homeostasis. *Archives of General Psychiatry* 9:457-473.

Glick, I.D., and Haley, J. (1971). *Family Therapy and Research.* An annotated bibilography of articles and books published 1950-1970. New York: Grune and Stratton.

Haley, J. (1955). Paradoxes in play, fantasy and psychotherapy. *Psychiatric Research Reports* 2:52-58..

Haley, J. (1959). The family of the schizophrenic: a model system. *Journal of Nervous and Mental Diseases* 129:357-374.

Haley, J. (1963). *Strategies of Psychotherapy.* New York: Grune and Stratton.

Haley, J. (1964). Research on family patterns: an instrument measurement. *Family Process* 3:41-65.

Haley, J. (1966). Toward a theory of pathological systems. In *Family Therapy and Disturbed Families,* ed. G. N. Zuk and I. Boszormenyi-Nagy. Palo Alto: Science and Behavior Books.

Haley, J. (1971). *Changing Family: A Family Therapy Reader.* New York: Grune and Stratton.

Jackson, D.D. (1957). The question of family homeostasis. *Psychiatric Quarterly* Suppl. 31:79-90.

Jackson, D.D., and Yalom, I. (1959). Family interaction, family homeostasis and some implications for conjoint family psychotherapy. In *Individual and Family Dynamics,* ed. J.H. Masserman. New York: Grune and Stratton.

Jackson, D.D., and Haley, J. (1963). Transference revisited. *Journal of Nervous and Mental Diseases* 137:363-371.

Jackson, D.D., ed. (1968). *Therapy, Communication and Change.* vol. 1, 2. Palo Alto: Science and Behavior Books.

Laing, R. D., and Esterson, A. (1964). *Sanity, Madness and the Family: Families of Schizophrenics.* London: Tavistock Publications.

Laing, R.D. (1969). *The Politics of the Family and Other Essays.* London: Tavistock Publications.

Lennard, H.L., and Bernstein, A. (1960). *The Anatomy of Psychotherapy: Systems of Communication and Expectation.* New York: Columbia University Press.

Lidz, T. (1963). *The Family and Human Adaptation.* New York: International Universities Press.

Lidz, T., Fleck, S., and Cornelison, A. (1965). *Schizophrenia and the Family.* New York: International Universities Press.

Pinna, L. (1971). *La Famiglia Esclusiva.* Bari: Laterza.

Rabkin, R. (1972). On books. *Family Process* 2:12.

Riskin, J. (1964).. Family interaction scales: a preliminary report. *Archives of General Psychiatry* 2:484–494.

Riskin, J. (1973). Methodology for studying family interaction. Archives of General Psychiatry. 8:343–348.

Russel, B. (1960). *Our Knowledge of the External World.* New York: Mentor Books.

Satir, V. (1964). *Conjoint Family Therapy.* Palo Alto: Science and Behavior Books.

Searles, H. (1959). The effort to drive the other person crazy: an element in the etiology and psychotherapy of schizophrenia. *British Journal of Medical Psychology* 32:1–18.

Searles, H. (1966). Feelings of guilt in the psychoanalyst. *Psychiatry* 29:319–323.

Selvini Palazzoli, M. (1970). Contesto e metacontesto nella psicoterapia della famiglia. *Arch. Psicol. Neurol. Psich.* 3:203–211.

Selvini Palazzoli, M. (1972). Racialism in the family. *The Human Context* 4:624–629.

Selvini Palazzoli, M. (1973). Il malato e la sua famiglia. *L'Ospedale Maggiore* 6:400–402.

Selvini Palazzoli, M. (1974). *Self Starvation: From the Intrapsychic to the Transpersonal Approach to Anorexia Nervosa.* London: Chaucer Publishing.

Selvini Palazzoli, M., Boscolo, L., Cecchin, G., and Prata, G. (1974). The treatment of children through brief therapy of their parents. *Family Process* 13:4.

Selvini Palazzoli, M. and Ferraresi, P. (1972). L'obsede et son conjoint. *Social Psychiatry* 7:90-97.

Shands, H.C. (1971). *The War with Words.* The Hague–Paris: Mouton.

Shapiro, R.J., and Budmann, S.H. (1973). Defection, termination and continuation in family and individual therapy. *Family Process* 1:55-67.

Sluzki, C., and Veron, E. (1971). The double-bind as a universal pathogenic situation. *Family Process* 10:397-417.

Sonne, J.C., Speck, R.V., and Jungreis, K.E. (1965). The absent member maneuver as a family resistance. In *Psychotherapy for the Whole Family*, Friedman, A.S. et al. New York: Springer.

Speer, D.C. (1970). Family system: morphostasis and morphogenesis—or is homeostasis enough? *Family Process* 9:259-278.

Spiegel, J.B., and Bell, N.M. (1959). Family of the psychotic patient. In *American Handbook of Psychiatry*, ed. S. Arieti. New York: Basic Books.

Watzlawick, P. (1964). *An Anthology of Human Comunication: Text and Tape.* Palo Alto: Science and Behavior Books.

Watzlawick, P., Beavin, J.H., and Jackson, D.D. (1967). *Pragmatics of Human Communication.* New York: Norton.

Watzlawick, P., Weakland, J.H., and Fish, R. (1974). *Change. Principles of Problem Formation and Problem Solution.* New York: Norton.

Weakland, J.H., Fish, R., Watzlawick, P. and Bodin, A.M. (1974). Brief therapy: focused problem resolution. *Family Process* 13.

Whitehead, A.N., and Russell, B. (1910-1913). *Principa Mathematica.* 3 vols. Cambridge: Cambridge University Press.

Wynne, L.C., and Thaler Singer, A. (1963-1965). Thought disorders and the family relations of schizophrenics. *Archives of General Psychiatry* 9:191-206; 12:187-212.

Wynne, L.C., Ryckoff, I.N., Day, I., and Hirsch, S.I. (1958). Pseudomutuality in the family relations of schizophrenics. *Psychiatry* 21:205-220.

Zuck, G.N., and Boszormenyi-Nagy, I. (1966). *Family Therapy and Disturbed Families.* Palo Alto: Science and Behavior Books.

INDEX